DEAD RECKONING

Learning from Accidents in the Outdoors

EMMA WALKER

Guilford, Connecticut

For Bix, my partner in all things

An imprint of The Rowman & Littlefield Publishing Group, Inc.
4501 Forbes Blvd., Ste. 200
Lanham, MD 20706
www.rowman.com
Falcon and FalconGuides are registered trademarks and Make Adventure Your Story is a
trademark of The Rowman & Littlefield Publishing Group, Inc.

Distributed by NATIONAL BOOK NETWORK

British Library Cataloguing in Publication Information available

Library of Congress Cataloging-in-Publication Data

Names: Walker, Emma, 1989– author.
Title: Dead reckoning : learning from accidents in the outdoors / Emma
   Walker.
Description: Guilford, Connecticut : FalconGuides, an imprint of the Rowman
   & Littlefield Publishing Group, Inc., [2021] | Includes bibliographical
   references. | Summary: "It's easier to stay alive if you know what's out
   there. That's the philosophy behind Dead Reckoning"— Provided by
   publisher.
Identifiers: LCCN 2020055300 (print) | LCCN 2020055301 (ebook) | ISBN
   9781493052783 (trade paperback) | ISBN 9781493052790 (epub)
Subjects: LCSH: Outdoor medical emergencies. | Outdoor medical
   emergencies—Prevention.
Classification: LCC RC88.9.O95 W35 2021 (print) | LCC RC88.9.O95 (ebook)
   | DDC 616.02/5—dc23
LC record available at https://lccn.loc.gov/2020055300
LC ebook record available at https://lccn.loc.gov/2020055301

Contents

Introduction

If you're using dead reckoning, things have gone terribly wrong.

That wasn't always the case. If you used dead reckoning to find your way home in a blizzard in the late nineteenth century, for example, you were on the cutting edge. You figured out approximately how far you now stood from the last place whose location you knew for certain—a road, the trail's intersection with a mountain stream—and about how long it would take you, moving at a given pace in a specific direction, to reach that spot.

More than 100 years later, we're nearly always surrounded by technology. We have GPS devices, smartphones that talk to satellites, up-to-date maps printed on waterproof paper, and reliable compasses. We have personal locator beacons and satellite phones we can use in case of emergency. We have marked, well-kept trails and expensive gear to keep us warm and dry.

Dead reckoning is what you use when all that fails.

It's what you use when your GPS can't get a signal and you've lost your map (or don't know how to read it) and your satellite phone isn't working. It's what you rely on when, despite that you're shivering and can't see a damn thing, you're pretty sure if you just walk south for three-quarters of a mile, you'll wind up someplace you know.

Even then, though, errors are cumulative. If you're off by a few hundred feet and don't see your mark, you'll pass it. What's beyond it? A cliff? Hundreds of miles of wilderness? Or if you assume you'll walk a mile in 15 minutes, but really it takes you 20 or 30—it's dark or blizzarding; your footing is uneven—what happens then?

It's easier not to think about those possibilities. It's much more pleasant to leave prepared for your next outing, whether it's a hike or a paddle or an overnight backpacking trip, and assume things will go as planned. If we spend all our time worrying about what *could happen*, it's overwhelming. It's easier to just stay home.

Of course, most of the time nothing goes wrong. The weather is fine. The bears keep their distance. The waves never become unmanageable. And even when things aren't quite what we expect, we're usually able to compensate. We pull out our rain jackets and use our bear spray and paddle back to shore when the whitecaps pick up.

But what happens when none of that works?

That's what this book is about—the times when things don't go as planned and people find themselves in way over their heads. Sometimes they're close calls (I've had plenty of those). Sometimes they end in tragedy. Dead reckoning is a navigational technique, but in this context, it's another way of preparing yourself. What do you do when the dire possibilities you know are associated with traveling in wild places come to fruition?

If you know what's out there, it's easier to stay alive.

This idea—that things are better and more manageable if I know the very worst of what might happen—has stuck with me all my life.

I have been fascinated by the morbid for as long as I can remember. Not in a creepy way—I didn't spend my adolescence harming animals; in fact, for most of my childhood, I was a strict vegetarian. (I possess only one hallmark of future serial killers: I remained a chronic bed-wetter until I was 12. This made me reluctant to attend sleepovers, but I am otherwise largely unaffected.)

But if I heard adults whispering in that telltale tone that indicated something awful had happened, I found myself dying to know more. I wanted details. Not the kid version—not "so-and-so has passed away"—I wanted to know how, exactly. If my campaign to hear What You'd Tell Another Adult worked, I would inevitably be deeply affected by it, often perseverating on the most gruesome plot points for days afterward.

Despite this insistence on hearing the worst things, I was a sensitive kid. During my elementary years, I regularly burst into my parents' room as my mother got ready for work. I would beg her not to make the commute; I was convinced she would be involved in a fatal car accident. When she came down with pneumonia—a potential way for my mom to die that had not yet occurred to me—midway through my third-grade year, a classmate asked me whether, if she died, my dad would still take me to my horseback riding lessons. I was so distraught at this prospect that my teacher sent me home for the day.

I could point to a dozen possibilities as to why I'm so interested in—and so worried about—death. None is related to trauma, at least not to my own. (I was lucky enough to have four living grandparents until I was 26.) But even in my quiet suburban neighborhood, horrible ways to die weren't far off.

The Columbine High School shooting happened when I was in third grade, a few weeks after my mom recovered from her pneumonia. It was in my school district, just 25 miles south of the nondescript Arvada, Colorado, street where I grew up. A day or two later, in the aftermath, our teacher gathered my class in a circle to answer questions. In my memory, she was holding a piece of paper, which I guess had a list of questions we might ask or information she was supposed to tell us (although I'm not sure, 20-odd years later, if any of that is true).

My third-grade teacher was probably about the age I am now. I remember her fondly. She calmly explained that something very sad had happened: Some young men who were very sick, she said, had shot some of their classmates and a teacher, and then they had taken their own lives. She let this sink in for a moment. I imagine this was the first time most of our eight- and nine-year-old brains had been asked to process something like this. She asked if anyone had any questions, and before I could stop myself—I said almost everything at that age before I could stop myself—I was raising my hand.

"Where did they shoot themselves?" I wanted to know.

My teacher was caught off guard. "In the library, I think?" she answered tentatively. I bet that question wasn't on her list.

I shook my head. I'd already heard on the news that it was in the library—my dad worked at a high school, and, understandably, he'd been standing in front of the TV in our living room watching the news almost constantly since the shooting. I, his precocious only child, had not been told to stay away (by then, he likely knew it was pointless to avoid the details, lest he look up and find me peering over the balcony into the den). So I sat on the couch behind him, glued to broadcasts about the tragedy. This was my only question that hadn't been answered: I wanted to know how the shooters had died.

"No, I mean where on their bodies?" I asked.

That definitely wasn't on the list.

"It doesn't really matter," she told me matter-of-factly, and of course she was right. I can't blame her for not wanting to explain the logistics of an unspeakably tragic event to her classroom of third graders.

But I can't have been the only kid who wanted to know. I was just the only one impulsive enough to ask.

Even then, I understood that most people aren't murdered. But in that moment, something crystallized for me. You simply never knew, I realized, when something awful might happen. All you could do was learn what had happened and try to understand *why*. You may not be able to avoid a terrible fate, I figured, but you could certainly go forth into the world feeling prepared.

In any case, I was an anxious kid. That's never really gone away, though I manage the cloud of anxiety, which constantly threatens to fully envelop me in a wild thunderstorm, much better now than I did at nine years old.

It occurs to me, sometimes, the irony that someone as anxious as myself has chosen to spend as much time as I have in objectively dangerous situations. I spent three winters in Alaska studying avalanches and decision-making. I've guided rafts down a section of whitewater containing sometimes-fatal Class IV rapids. I regularly tie into a rope to climb mountains and traverse heavily crevassed glaciers. The list goes on.

People often ask me if I'm scared in those situations. Sure I am.

I'm as afraid of heights as anyone with a lick of common sense. It is objectively scary to think about being buried in an avalanche or drowning or falling off a cliff to one's death. Most of the time, I am so supremely focused on what I'm doing that thoughts of death are too far away to really scare me. When they do occur, I'm able to rationalize, for the most part. I can weigh the risk—how likely is it that this thing I'm doing will kill me?—using science and past experience.

That, and if I never did anything I was afraid to do, I'd never do anything at all.

It's that attitude ("I might as well try it") that's made me a dabbler. A season of raft guiding here, a stint in Alaska there; a handful of days or weeks spent at a smattering of parks and crags around the western United States.

That's what this book does, too. It doesn't expect you to be an expert at any one thing, because most of us aren't. Most outdoor recreators like to hike and maybe occasionally climb or paddle but aren't planning to quit their day jobs to do them full-time anytime soon. Accident narratives should be accessible to those who aren't experts, too. The thing that ties all the narratives in this book together, really, is the draw to understand what could happen, coupled with the hope that we can avoid it.

I spent most of my early adulthood stopping myself from asking questions that would have helped me better understand the morbid details. I learned in third grade, and many times thereafter, that asking someone to describe a terrible accident was not generally considered a sign that I was well adjusted. As interest in true crime becomes more mainstream, it's become clear to me for the first time that I am not, in fact, alone in that regard.

Each chapter in this book contains a personal narrative about somewhere I've been or something I've done. I'm far from perfect. I've made plenty of mistakes. Some are more recent and more embarrassing than others. I'm sharing them with you in the hopes that you can learn from them.

In all the time I've been working and recreating outside, I've been very lucky. I've had some close calls—some I should have seen coming, others I couldn't possibly have avoided except by not being in the wrong place at the wrong time—but I've always come out unscathed. (Rest assured that I'm knocking on wood as I write this.) If there's one thing I've learned, it's that luck favors the prepared. That's where the rest of each chapter comes in.

As I worked on this book, I consulted experts. I read hundreds of accident accounts in newspapers, magazines, and other books. I pored over maps and looked at weather patterns. In each chapter that follows, I've included details from some of the less lucky folks I talked to and read about.

At the end of each chapter, I've included a section called "Lessons Learned." Here, I've boiled down everything I've learned and read and heard and experienced so you can prepare yourself before you head outside. After all, the risks are great, but so are the rewards. When it's all said and done, I think taking some calculated risks for the sake of adventure is worth it.

If you don't want to read the gruesome details, this is probably a good stopping point for you. If you're like me, though, and you can't look away—this book is for you.

LAND ACKNOWLEDGMENT

EVERY INCIDENT DESCRIBED IN THIS BOOK TAKES PLACE ON LAND that has been stewarded for many generations by indigenous people. Many of them took place on what I'm referring to as "public land." While this is true in the sense that this land is now open for recreation to the American public, in many cases, it was usurped from people whose ancestors had lived there for centuries and remains unceded territory. I respectfully acknowledge the indigenous nations on whose land I traveled in the essays that follow:

Chapter 1: Shoshone-Bannock and Cheyenne people

Chapter 2: Shoshone-Bannock, Eastern Shoshone, Cheyenne, Dena'ina Ełnena, Ahtna Nenn', Apsaalooké (Crow), and Očeti Šakówiŋ (Sioux) people

Chapter 3: Núu-agha-tʉvʉ-pʉ (Ute) and Cheyenne people

Chapter 4: Cheyenne and Núu-agha-tʉvʉ-pʉ (Ute) people

Chapter 5: Kanaka ʻŌiwi people

Chapter 6: Anishinabewaki and Očeti Šakówiŋ (Sioux) people

Chapter 7: Dena'ina Ełnena, Cheyenne, and Núu-agha-tʉvʉ-pʉ_ (Ute) people

Chapter 8: Puyallup and Nisqually people

Chapter 9: Núu-agha-tʉvʉ-pʉ (Ute), Hopi, Diné, Pueblos, and Havasupai people

Chapter 10: Tanana and Alutiiq (Sugpiaq) people

For more information on the specific people on whose ancestral land you're traveling, you can visit https://native-land.ca.

CHAPTER ONE

CSI: Yellowstone

IT'S JUST AFTER 2:00 P.M. ON NEW YEAR'S DAY, AND MY HUSBAND, Bix, and I are cross-country skiing into a thicket of trees in the Gneiss Creek drainage, about two miles from the Yellowstone National Park boundary. Nighttime temperatures have been dipping down to 20 degrees below zero, but now, just after solar noon, the sun bounces off untouched snow to warm our faces, still tender with windburn from yesterday's outing.

Our plan is to camp at or near an established backcountry site about another three miles down the trail, where we'll escape the constant low hum of two-stroke engines for a quiet night under the stars. We're carrying everything we'll need for a relatively comfortable night of winter camping—it's all jammed into our 60-liter backpacks and a duffel bag lashed to a tricked-out kiddie sled.

Despite my insistence that I'm more than capable of hauling the sled, Bix is the one pulling it. Normally I'm in front, because putting the slowest skier in the lead makes it easier to stick together. With the extra weight, he is, even with his long legs, moving considerably slower than me. I don't mind taking up the rear for once, and the arrangement works fine until he stops short halfway down the drainage, causing me to lurch forward cartoonishly, barely catching myself on my ski poles.

I'm about to launch an as-yet-unheard string of curse words when I realize he hasn't just zoned out on the scenery for the sixth or seventh time today.

He mutters something incomprehensible under his breath, doing his best to back away from whatever he's just seen. It would be kind of funny, watching him try to backtrack uphill on skis, the sled slamming into his boots with each step, if only he didn't sound so alarmed.

I begin to conjure the possibilities. In this part of the world, grizzlies are typically at the top of my list of concerns, but the bears will still be asleep for another two months, at least. A bison? No—we're too far off the beaten path; they're grazing in a valley a dozen miles away.

I can't see what's got Bix's tongue, so I ski off the trail to get around the unwieldy sled.

Before me lies one of the most gruesome scenes I've ever encountered. It looks like something from a slasher movie. A trail of blood and hair winds its way to a freshly killed elk, whose final resting place is less than 10 feet off the trail.

Yellowstone National Park occupies nearly 3,500 square miles of wilderness. Boasting some of North American's most charismatic megafauna—it's the only place where bison have lived continuously since prehistoric times—the park encompasses most of northwestern Wyoming, occasionally spilling over its borders into Montana and Idaho.

It was the bison, if I'm being honest, that brought me to Yellowstone. I had read, years earlier, that bison use their broad, hairy faces to brush snow away from their favorite grasses all winter. This technique allows Yellowstone's resident bison to hardily graze their way through the Madison Valley—whose namesake river never freezes, thanks to its geothermal sourcing—even as the mercury drops tens of degrees below zero. I'd wanted to see one of these giant Bovidae, preferably in their frosty winter state, ever since.

On our first morning in West Yellowstone, Montana, Bix and I waited for the temperature to reach a balmy zero. We piled into our Forester, which was reluctant to start after so cold a night, and coaxed it across town to the visitor center, where we would pick up the backcountry permit we needed for our Gneiss Creek outing the following day.

The park's backcountry rangers are understandably skeptical when someone announces they'd like to spend a night out in subzero temperatures in January. It's uncommon enough that you have to call ahead so a law enforcement ranger can meet you at the visitor center to issue a permit, for which you must have a detailed plan. Ranger Rick seemed satisfied by our combined winter camping experience, and soon we were hashing out the finer points of fish scale versus waxed skis.

Before he could print our permit, though, his radio crackled to life: We'd have to come back later, he said; there was a CPR in progress in the park.

"*Bison goring!*" I hissed to Bix, who pointedly ignored my supposition. I raised an eyebrow. "I hope we see one."

The ranger at the desk suggested a diversion while we waited out the medical emergency. Twenty minutes later, we were swishing along the Madison River toward Seven Mile Bridge, spotting bald eagles, countless swans, a bobcat, and, much to my delight, four bison.

I was so excited, in fact, that despite my usual consternation at the countless wildlife-related injuries in Yellowstone each year, I had trouble restraining myself from approaching them to get a good picture. This temptation is, apparently, a common one.

"To many Yellowstone visitors," Lee H. Whittlesey writes of the bison in *Death in Yellowstone: Accidents and Foolhardiness in the*

First National Park, "it is not a genuine living, breathing creature. Instead, it is a painting, a symbol of a vanished past, a vignette of nineteenth-century America, but certainly nothing real."

To date, Yellowstone bison have killed only two people—a surprisingly small number considering the number of gorings reported since the park's establishment. The fatalities occurred in 1971 and 1983, both of them when the victims approached lone bulls with the intention of snapping a photo.

More than 50 people were gored in the 1980s and 90s, almost always because they'd gotten too close to the bison in question. The number of incidents has dropped not because bison are increasingly tame, but because the park has taken additional precautions to warn visitors not to approach them. These creatures can weigh upward of 2,000 pounds, and Whittlesey, a decades-long resident of the area, reports having watched them charge the van-sized snowcoaches transporting visitors throughout the park in the winter. Bison are not to be trifled with.

By the time we made it back to the closed-down entrance station—visiting a national park in the dead of winter really makes you feel like you're getting away with something—the sun had begun its retreat behind the Gallatin Range. We pulled up to the visitor center on the edge of town just as a snowcoach full of amateur photographers sputtered its way into the parking lot, and I couldn't help but feel a little smug that I'd get to explore the park sans company of motorists the next day.

Early the next morning, we chatted with another ranger, who double-checked our plan and sent us on our merry way.

"Happy New Year!" she ended our exchange. "Enjoy your night out!"

Surveying the scene in front of me, I can practically hear the *Law and Order* theme song. Neither of us speaks for what seems like ages, until I can't stand it any longer.

"What did this?" I ask, though I'm already scanning the crime scene for clues.

The trail, such as it is, cuts through a clearing from the top of the gully to the bottom, bisecting a gentle hillside. A hundred feet above us is the top of a knoll, populated by shivery quaking aspens. Across the little drainage are dense trees, coated in hard snow the consistency of icing on a ginger snap. The only trees anywhere near the trail are two lodgepole pines 10 feet below us, one of which shelters the remains of the elk.

In graduate school, I spent a great deal of time and energy thinking about the complex scientific properties of snow, marveling at its viscoelasticity and ability to conduct and insulate. I know the ingredients of an avalanche—a slab, a bed surface, a trigger—and how to identify various types of snow crystals. I spend an inordinate amount of time thinking about what it's like to be caught and buried in an avalanche; this causes me to look up at the slope above us and determine, based on a rough internal inclinometer calibrated by many years of looking at slope angles, that it's probably not steep enough to slide.

What I don't take enough time to appreciate is the way snow can tell a story. Here's what it tells us today:

The tracks leading to the elk carcass plunge deep into the snow, the work of an ungulate on its long last legs. They stagger downhill, marking the path of least resistance with tiny droplets of now-frozen blood. This poor creature wasn't giving up easily, but it didn't have far to go.

Another set of prints runs parallel to the elk tracks. Unlike the elk, the creature that made these tracks wasn't in a hurry. It followed the elk downhill slowly—calculatedly. The narrow, perfectly spaced pawprints are in stark contrast to the elk's panicked, uneven pace. They spoon their victim's tracks down to the tree before us, where what's left of the elk now rests.

Surrounding the carcass are prints of all shapes and sizes: Magpie feet, marks that mimic the way a bear slashes a tree trunk (raven wings), timid coyote tracks. Even a good-sized badger has lumbered over for its share of the bounty.

Across the gully and trailing uphill into the woods is a set of tracks matching that of the predator. Each print is the size of my fist. It could easily be confused with the print of a domestic dog, except for one teeny detail: Those perfectly round toe pads don't have claw marks in front of them. Unlike dogs, cats keep their claws retracted unless they're, say, killing an elk.

The feline's tracks are just wide enough to accommodate the detail that quickens my heart rate—it's as if the creature that left them was dragging something behind it.

Something like a tail.

This isn't a harmless, tailless bobcat. It's a cougar. An enormous, watching-us-right-now, finally-got-an-elk-and-we're-keeping-him-from-eating-it cougar.

Startled, we look around. Of course we can't see anything. You don't see a cougar unless it wants you to, probably because it's about to make you into charcuterie.

Cougars, catamounts, mountain lions, pumas, panthers—call them what you like, depending where you live; a *Puma concolor* by any other name is still an apex predator. Its interactions with humans are fewer and farther between than most of the heavy hitters. You hear about bear maulings and shark attacks (humans are usually at least partially culpable), but cougar encounters are quite rare.

When I was in college and living in Boulder, Colorado, I read David Baron's *The Beast in the Garden*, which takes place in the foothills just outside of town. It scared me off hiking by myself for a good six months. Cougars had finally gained protected status in the American West after more than half a century of bounties for their carcasses. This was an overblown response to intermittent livestock killings, not discontinued in Colorado until 1965, by which time over 1,700 animals had been killed in exchange for monetary rewards. The renewed success of the mountain lion, unfortunately, coincides with incessant urban sprawl. The mountain residents concerned about cougars encroaching on their space are, ironically and literally, in the lion's den.

The most dangerous creatures, of course, are the individuals we've habituated. But despite their close quarters, mountain lions rarely attack healthy, fully grown humans. They certainly don't do it in broad daylight, generally speaking.

Still, the culmination of Baron's book is the 1991 death of teenager Scott Lancaster, a talented cyclist and high school student in Idaho Springs who was killed by a mountain lion as he went for a jog in the middle of a school day. His body was so badly mutilated when searchers finally found it that authorities initially suspected foul play.

Incidents like Lancaster's death are exceedingly rare, but this is cold comfort for unattended pets and small children (or, as it turns out, the fledgling outdoorswoman I was at 20). Still, I reasoned from my standpoint at the Gneiss Creek drainage, where I couldn't shake the feeling of being watched, odds are good that a wild, non-habituated cougar is much more frightened of a pair of humans with skis and sleds than said humans are of it. In this case, that was really saying something.

Despite our assuredness that the owner of this carcass isn't going to leap on us out of nowhere—I envision myself fending it off with my ski poles, hoping I come off as tough, rather than ridiculous— we don't exactly want to linger in the clearing.

Bix starts off down the hill, the sled bobbing on and off the trail behind him. He stops again and points wordlessly at the trail in front of him.

The cat has followed the trail down the hill. This makes sense; it's much easier to walk on snow packed down by humans on skis than to finish each step submerged in feet of unconsolidated snow. The prints sink deep into the snow—the cat is heavy. It would have to be to take out a full-grown elk. Bits of blood and fur, the occasional squirt of cat urine, which smells just as strongly of ammonia as that of a domestic feline—it was here within the last couple of hours.

We come around the corner at the bottom of the hill, looking for a place to stop and discuss our new plan. A few hundred yards ahead, we'll need to cross an open stream, landing ourselves in a meadow with a relatively clear view of our surroundings.

Before we can get to the stream, we encounter another pair of tracks: The elk crossed the trail here, too, heading up the hill toward its final destination, its gait already faltering. Our eyes follow the tracks to their origin and see signs of a scuffle—displaced snow everywhere, the morbid snow angel of a beast about to leave the corporeal world. There's an old set of cat tracks alongside it, stalking it up the hill, and then—

Fresh tracks. Everything around them is covered in feathery hoar frost, but these are totally undisturbed. They're practically steaming.

The cat was ahead of us, but it doubled back, probably when it heard us approach its cache.

I've suspected this from the moment we identified the tracks, but my fears are confirmed. It's watching us from somewhere up the hill.

We stop to catch our breath (or, in my case, breathe at all) across the little creek. Bix rummages through his backpack and pulls out a thermos of coffee. It's supposed to get down to 15 below tonight. We've both slept out in colder, but we've made a Plan B, anyway: If either of our old cold injuries—his a couple of fingers, mine a few toes—starts to look worse for wear, we'll simply ski back out after dinner.

"Cold injury" is a way to say frostbite without alarming your mother, but that's what it refers to. (Trench foot and the very gross-sounding chilblains are also cold injuries.) Bix got his in his late teens, when he did a solo ski trip through the Porcupine Mountains on Michigan's Upper Peninsula. Once you've frostbitten a body part, it's much more susceptible to similar injury. His fingertips and the end of his nose occasionally turn white and waxy now.

I got mine when I was 23, on a month-long excursion into the Talkeetna Mountains in Alaska—we woke up one morning and the temperature had dropped more than 60 degrees overnight. There is a common misconception that once it gets cold enough, the difference between, say, 20 and 40 degrees below zero is negligible. I (and my right big toe, in particular) can confirm without a shadow of a doubt that this is utterly untrue: 20 degrees below zero is cold, sure, but 40 below is a hell of a lot colder.

As my toes warmed up in the days after I came out of the Talkeetnas, I experienced what ice climbers often call the "screaming barfies." Charming, but it's also the most descriptive way to convey what it feels like when one's extremities begin to thaw out. As a frostbite specialist in Anchorage would later tell me, I'm lucky I lost only a toenail, not the whole toe.

Frostbite is front of mind, given our collective experience with cold injury, but the effects of cold can cause one to lose a lot more than a digit or even a limb. In Yellowstone, where the nighttime temperature we're looking at tonight is balmy in comparison to occasional cold snaps of 60 below, hypothermia is a very real possibility.

At least a dozen people have frozen to death in Yellowstone. Several of these were in the late nineteenth century. It's easy to chalk these early deaths by exposure up to ill-suited winter cloth-ing, but freezing deaths haven't stopped altogether in the last few decades. A park visitor died of exposure after separating from his wife on the frontcountry trail to Artist Point in the spring of 1999; a decade later, a Gardiner resident attempted to walk home after crashing his truck and made it just a mile and a half before he suc-cumbed to temperatures of 23 degrees below zero.

I say "at least" a dozen people because official statistics don't include those who are missing and presumed dead. A young man who vanished on a hunting trip in Yellowstone in February 1983 was missing for seven years before hunters finally found his body. A two-week search at the time of his disappearance turned up nothing, thanks to snow that reached searchers' waists. He probably died of hypothermia, which is also what very likely happened to the man who went missing somewhere off the Hellroaring trailhead in the spring of 1991. Of course, since he's never been found, it's impossible to say with any certainty. There is no shortage of ways to die in Yellowstone National Park.

Spend enough time outside, and you'll discover there's always a reason to come up with a backup plan. Now, though, we don't relish the idea of tromping up the drainage at dusk, when our crepuscular friend will be feeling friskiest. This is to say nothing of my disinter-est in being anywhere near the kill site after dark.

With our escape route cut off, we table our disappointment, stuff our parkas into our backpacks, and get ready for the snow to tell us one more story.

I'm always hearing people say they get mixed up about how to react to various animal encounters: "Do I play dead or fight back?" they ask. I often wonder if I'd have the presence of mind to remember how to react to a grizzly versus a black bear, should one actually attack me, but the protocol for mountain lion confrontations is, thanks to my wide-eyed reading of the aforementioned Baron book, etched permanently in my mind.

Talk loudly. Better yet, yell. Give it an escape route. Don't turn your back. Make yourself big. Raise your arms. Bare your teeth. Stare it right in the eyes. Don't look away. Fight back. Protect your head and neck. Go for its eyes.

Basically: become a cougar. Not that your inner cougar is any match for the 180-pound genuine article, of course. They have more practice.

We make good time through the clearing and get to within spitting distance of the park boundary in just under half an hour. No cougars. I am nonetheless thoroughly shaken up. Bix suggests we stop for another coffee break and I readily agree: I want to tell him something that will make his stomach churn.

"Wanna hear something that'll make you feel like puking?" he asks.

"You first," I tell him.

Our skis had erased the cat tracks from the trail as we slid down the drainage. As we'd headed back up, Bix, skiing in front me, looked down and noticed something odd. The trail was not smooth and blank, as it should have been if the last creatures to use it had been wearing skis. It had a fresh set of prints, this one leading back up the hill—same direction as us.

While we regrouped on the other side of the creek, the mountain lion had doubled back from its perch at the top of the knoll and followed the trail back up to the cache. It had been waiting for us.

Indeed, this story makes me feel a little nauseous, especially since I have corroborating evidence: As we crested the hill at the top of the drainage, out of sight but no more than 200 yards from the carcass, I heard a scuffle. In my hyper-alert state, I jerked my head around to see what it was.

A conspiracy of ravens scattered into the bluebird sky, squawking in protest at having been displaced from their prize.

I don't know of much that'll scare a group of scavenging birds away as quickly as the sudden appearance of a cat, though this was on a much larger scale than your typical Tweety-fleeing-Sylvester-in-the-window scenario.

"And don't come back," I picture the cougar telling us, shaking its fist in our direction.

After processing our near miss over our now-cold coffee, we skied to the car and headed back to West Yellowstone. The ranger we'd talked to that morning had asked us to call when we were out of the field. Her alarm was palpable when she answered our call, placed 18 hours earlier than she'd expected, on the first ring. She asked us to meet her at the visitor center, where we marked the location of the cache on a map and showed her an array of grisly photos.

"The Resource Management guys are going to *love these*," she told us, unable to conceal a tinge of envy. "Man, we never get to see cougars!"

It's true: In all our collective time spent in the wilderness—which, between Bix and me, is many years—neither of us had ever seen a mountain lion outside of captivity.* We don't know many people who have.

I could say we're lucky not to have been attacked, and that's certainly true. But there's more to it than that. Ungulates make up some 99 percent of a cougar's winter diet, so there are ostensibly scenes like this all over Yellowstone National Park each year—most far from the places humans find themselves on New Year's Day.

In that sense, we were lucky to have experienced this incredibly intimate aspect of the ecosystem we chose to travel in. (On the other hand, I'm also very glad we weren't there a few hours earlier.)

---

* Ironically—or perhaps not, given the intersection of habituated cougars and urban sprawl—Bix would see a mountain lion around six months later on North Table Mountain, just a few blocks from our apartment in Golden. It followed him for 100 yards or so and eventually lost interest, but not without giving him a good scare.

The snow writes the stories of these everyday triumphs and trage-
dies, two sides of the same ecological coin, if only you know how
to read them.

LESSONS LEARNED

- **Don't approach wildlife.** No photo—not even one of gigantic frosty bison—is worth a bison goring. That's true for you,
  and also for the animals. It takes a tremendous amount of
  energy just to survive a Yellowstone winter (though this is
  true in other landscapes, too). Elk, moose, deer, and bison
  work hard to stay alive when resources dwindle during the
  colder months, and they can't afford the energy it takes to
  charge humans when we approach too closely. That photo
  could cost a critter its life.

- **Know what wildlife you might encounter—and how to
  behave if you do.** The cast of characters depends on when
  and where you're going. Bears aren't active in the winter, but
  if we'd headed to Yellowstone in the summertime, we'd have
  had a whole different setup (one that included bear spray
  and the knowledge to use it). It's also worth brushing up on
  your predator responses. Sure, there's a chance you'll be too
  panicked to remember what to do in the moment. But being
  prepared can't hurt, and it might very well help.

- **Have an exit strategy.** I'm constantly running through
  worst-case scenarios in my head. One upside to being an
  anxious person comes into play when I'm making backcountry plans; this tendency of mine means I'm prepared for any
  number of possibilities. What are the risks—will it be terribly cold? Is there a river crossing? Is the area known for bear
  activity? Making a list of risks allows me to make Plan B
  (and C, and D, and so forth) accordingly.

- **Pay attention.** This is a matter of safety—although in this particular case, even if we hadn't been paying attention, it would have been hard to miss a mutilated elk carcass. But it's also a matter of connecting to a place. The end result would have been the same whether we'd turned tail the moment we saw a freshly killed animal or stuck around to figure out what killed the elk and how it happened: We wouldn't have spent that night out. But by observing our surroundings carefully, we learned a valuable lesson about the critters that inhabit that landscape, how to identify them, and when to throw in the towel. They've stuck with us ever since.

CHAPTER TWO

Bear Bait

THE WEST YELLOWSTONE VISITOR CENTER HAS A SMALL OFFICE in the back of the building where backcountry visitors can pick up their permits. The walls are adorned with the accoutrements you might expect—maps, brochures, newspaper articles about the national park.

Tacked to a crowded corkboard is a cutout from a magazine featuring two large bears surrounded by lush greenery. Some clever ranger has scrawled over the image in permanent marker.

"Are we griz or black bears?" the one on the left asks its companion.

"Does it really matter?" the other bear counters.

If I had to sum up my philosophy on bears with a single quip, this would be it. There are ways to tell bear species apart—geography, color, size, and so forth—but we'll get to that later. What it really comes down to is that it doesn't matter all that much what type of bear you encounter. Mostly it just matters that you avoid them when possible and know what to do if you do encounter one (or, worse, two).

I grew up in Colorado, where we only have black bears. I often joke that they're essentially large raccoons: You don't really want to run into one, but they're basically harmless, and they mostly want to eat your garbage. This is an oversimplification, of course;

habituated black bears are responsible for more predatory attacks than other bear species.* Still, there's a kernel of truth to this joke: You're far less likely to encounter a bear of any kind if you store food and dispose of trash properly.

In any case, this meant that I was relatively clueless about bears when I moved to Alaska. That was mostly fine, since I primarily lived there in the winter, when grizzly and brown bears are snug in their dens.† The closest I came to a bear encounter in Alaska was, years after I'd moved away, reading an *Anchorage Daily News* article about an acquaintance from my alma mater being attacked by a bear in southeast Alaska. (Thankfully, he survived.)

Most of the grizzly bears I've seen have been in the Tetons, not far from the West Yellowstone Visitor Center.

Days after I finished my first year of graduate school, I moved home to Colorado for the summer. The National Park Service job I'd intended to work in Alaska for the season had been rendered moot by a government shutdown, and I was left scrambling for summer employment. I landed a job at a nonprofit organization in my home state, where I worked as a camp counselor for eight- to twelve-year-olds on their first overnight camping trips.

The job meant working 24-hour-long camps, followed by debriefs and cleanup, so it was emotionally and physically draining. The upside was that this meant my co-counselors and I typically had three-day weekends, and we spent every single one of them traipsing around the mountains of Colorado and Wyoming.

---

* Excluding the polar bear, which I've left out of this chapter intentionally. The average adventurer is not likely to encounter a polar bear, a species that dwells only in the very high arctic. Even as polar bears move farther south and begin to interbreed with grizzly bears, producing the "pizzly bear" or "Nanaluk" (I prefer "Grohlar bear," but no one else seems to find my grunge rock/bear puns as clever as I do). While this is truly a terrifying prospect, most North Americans are not at risk of an encounter in the sparsely populated regions those hybrids inhabit. If you're heading into polar bear country, you should do more specific research on what polar bear avoidance entails.

† I did see a large bear one April afternoon, about 30 yards away as I hiked the approach to a climb off the Seward Highway. My partner and I hightailed it out of there, figuring we'd save climbing for another day.

We had a particularly long stretch of time off during the week of the Fourth of July. The moment camp ended, my coworkers and I loaded up our cars and headed north to Jackson.

Predictably on the busiest holiday weekend of the season, all the camping in and immediately surrounding Grand Teton National Park was full. We hadn't planned quite that far ahead. Still, we managed to find some free dispersed camping off Highway 191, just southeast of Hoback Shield, a popular sport climbing area.

We arrived just as dusk was fading to darkness and set up camp at an unoccupied spot. There was no firepit or picnic table or bear storage box here, just a crude fire ring and a few patches of dusty earth where tents had clearly been set up many times before.

A few hours later, our group of five sleepily piled into the Subaru Forester we'd borrowed from my dad (none of us had a vehicle that was both reliable enough to drive 500-plus miles *and* could fit five people), which we drove through Jackson and into the national park. We parked at Lupine Meadows and began the long trudge up the Garnet Canyon Trail, the approach to the Grand and Middle Tetons, around 3:30 a.m., the trail lit only by the stars and our headlamps.

As it turns out, I was not the only one with zero grizzly bear experience and disproportionate concern about them. As we hiked up the trail toward our intended climb, surrounded by pitch-black night, we stopped short almost constantly.

"Did you hear that?" someone would ask, ready to deploy the bear spray.

Inevitably, a deer would leap out of the bushes and bound up the hill. We'd be relieved momentarily, then settle right back into walking on eggshells.

I guess it was better to be overzealous than unprepared. The only real consequence of our worrying was that our constant stops meant it took us twice the time it should have to hike to the boulder field where the scramble up the Middle Teton begins. By the time we arrived, it was fully light outside, and there was no way we'd have time to make the summit and be back below tree line before an afternoon thunderstorm predictably rolled in. Instead, we took our time strolling back down the trail and bellied up to the bar at Dornan's, just down the road from Lupine Meadows in Moose. A few hours later, we watched a truly awe-inspiring storm over our intended summit from the bar's patio, reminding us that we'd at least done one thing right that day.

Hiking in a group of five chatty twentysomethings isn't a guarantee that one won't encounter a bear, but it's pretty close—who wouldn't steer clear? We were paranoid, sure, and there's a solid middle ground somewhere between charging up the trail with no bear spray and our debilitating concern.

In fact, as we'd soon discover, we were far more likely to encounter a bear at our makeshift campsite. In my memory, we were pretty good about cleaning up our cooking equipment and garbage and storing them in my dad's car before we turned in each night. But we weren't the first people to use this spot, which was situated at the edge of a little seasonal stream and almost entirely surrounded by willows.

If you read that description and thought, *Hmm, that sounds like the kind of place a bear might like to hang out,* you'd be exactly right. Why this didn't occur to any of us—a group of outdoor educators who'd lived in notoriously bear-happy places like Montana and Alaska—I cannot possibly say, except that we all probably assumed someone else would say something if there was a problem.

After a summer of working outside and camping together, we'd all gotten used to talking about our various bowel movements. So when Pat grabbed a roll of toilet paper one evening around dusk and wandered off into the willows, no one thought much of it.

That is, until we heard a bloodcurdling shriek and Pat came racing back into our campsite, holding his pants up, with his curly red hair looking even wilder than usual and all the color drained from his face.

He started to stammer about a bear, and we all looked up in time to see the willows rustling as it shuffled away.

"A bear . . . literally . . . scared the shit out of Pat!" Bix snorted between peals of laughter. Today, you can remind Pat of this incident (Bix likes to do this regularly) and you'll get a chuckle out of him. But at the time, he was understandably pretty shaken.

Somehow, it still didn't occur to us to move campsites that night. At some point in the wee hours, Bix got up to pee and came rushing back into our tent, having spooked another (or maybe the same) bear.

We didn't see a single bear when we were fully prepared to but encountered two in the span of 12 hours when we least expected it. A little ironic, maybe, but that's how it goes with bears: Very often, humans encounter them because of something we've done or neglected to do, not because they're vicious predators craving human flesh.

I've always heard the term "habituated" used to refer to dangerous bears—"a fed bear is a dead bear" is conventional wisdom. Actually, says bear biologist Wes Larson, habituation doesn't necessarily mean a bear is aggressive.

"'Habituated' just means a bear is used to human presence," explains Larson, who specializes in human-bear conflicts. He points to Timothy Treadwell, famously the subject of Werner Herzog's 2005 *Grizzly Man*. Over the course of 13 summers, bears at Katmai National Park and Preserve got used to having him around. Most realized he wasn't prey. (Unfortunately, being used to human presence doesn't necessarily mean avoiding or peacefully coexisting with humans, and Treadwell was mauled to death at his campsite in 2003.)

It's a spectrum, Larson says. Bears in some remote corner of the Alaskan wilderness who've never encountered a human are on one end. Then you've got habituated bears—those who spend a lot of time in the vicinity of the popular hiking trails of Grand Teton National Park (or near a mountain town like Durango or Missoula), maybe, who are used to seeing humans. Generally, they'd prefer to stay away; they might notice you, but they'll probably continue whatever it is they're doing. Farther along on the spectrum is food conditioning.

A "problem bear," the term often used to describe an individual who won't stop breaking into dumpsters or harassing campers in their tents, is likely a food-conditioned bear.

"A bear that breaks into someone's campsite and eats their food has just learned that they can get this really calorie-dense food," Larson says. "It's a huge payoff for so little effort. And that's when they start doing really non-beary things."

That's when they interact with humans, in other words. That's when they get into trouble.

Two years after that trip to the Tetons, Bix was still working as the lead instructor at the overnight camp where we'd met. I'd just finished training to be a raft guide, which hadn't turned out to be the mellow post–grad school summer job I'd been counting on. When I needed a break, I'd come up and volunteer for a day or two to clear my head.

Little kids get up really early, especially when they're giddy to have survived their first-ever camping trip. This meant we instructors needed to be up and at 'em by 5:30 a.m. or so, and while I like a good sunrise as much as the next person, I was usually pretty bleary-eyed as I made my way up to the kitchen (the rickety back room of one of the only structures on the property, a long-neglected bunkhouse with no running water) to start coffee.

One morning, I turned up in the kitchen to find Bix and another counselor, Adam, standing dumbstruck in the doorway. They didn't say a word when I walked in, just sipped their coffee, wide-eyed. I poured myself a cup and looked around at the wreckage.

Shattered glass from a broken window littered the floor. Boxes of the dried food we served—macaroni and powdered cheese, hot chocolate mix—had been ripped open and scattered around the room. Chocolatey pawprints wandered across the cheap linoleum, eventually leaving via the now-open window.

Someone had spotted a bear and a pair of cubs a couple of weeks earlier at the camp's dumpster, which had then been reinforced with a lock. We'd figured the kitchen, makeshift though it was, would be sufficient food storage. It had a locking door, and the windows were four feet or so off the ground.

But by the time camp started up that summer, the bear who broke into our kitchen had likely been breaking into dumpsters and garbage cans for years. She'd learned that humans mean food, and with two little cubs to look out for, she was probably willing to push the envelope for some relatively easy calories.

I'm grateful none of us encountered her in the kitchen that night—who knows what would've happened if I'd shown up midway through her midnight snack with a gaggle of homesick tweens.

"A bear in a campsite isn't going to act like a bear in the wild," Larson says. "All the rules are out the window—it's a bear that's going to act much more aggressively."

For the rest of that summer, nighttime bathroom trips meant taking groups of three or four students at a time. Counselors slept with miniature air horns in their tent vestibules. We didn't see the bear again. Maybe the effects of a pound of hot chocolate mix and most of a bottle of hot sauce didn't sit well with her, or maybe she broke into the wrong neighbor's dumpster and got relocated or killed.

It bothers me to think our camp could have helped her food conditioning along, though by the time a bear is breaking windows, it may very well be too late to break the cycle.

Responsible food storage might prevent a bear encounter in camp, but it doesn't do much to help you on the trail.

One principle does remain the same, regardless of whether you're traveling in grizzly or black bear country: Your best bet to avoid a negative interaction with a bear is to avoid seeing one in the first place. Most bears don't want to encounter humans, so if you can give them some warning that you're heading up the trail, they'll likely cede it.

You can do this by hiking in a group and making a lot of noise, as my co-counselors and I did on the way to Garnet Canyon that summer. Singing to oneself is a totally reasonable way to let bears know you're coming. (Anecdotally, I've found that bears steer clear of Foo Fighters lyrics, probably because they, too, are afraid to run into a Grohlar bear. I'm just saying.) If you can't bring yourself to sing, an occasional "Hey, bear!" shout is the bare minimum.

It also makes sense to think carefully about when and where you're hiking. Alongside a noisy stream alone at dawn or dusk? Very likely place to spook a bear who can't hear you.

In July 2011, students and instructors on a 30-day National Outdoor Leadership School (NOLS) course made their way through Alaska's Talkeetna Mountains. A group of seven students—an appropriate group size for the area, since it's unheard of for groups of four or more people to be attacked by a bear—hiked down a stream. The student in the lead spotted what he thought was a bale of hay in the stream ahead; by the time he realized it was in fact a blonde-colored grizzly sow (probably protecting a cub), it was too late for the two group members who carried bear spray to dig it out from the bottoms of their packs.

It's exceedingly rare for bears to attack people traveling in groups of this size. Perhaps the bear, caught off guard, only saw the group's leader when she charged, then realized there were other threats to neutralize. In all, four of the seven students were mauled. Thanks to quick thinking and good wilderness first aid skills, all of them survived.

This incident happened about a year before I moved to Alaska. I didn't hear about it at the time because on the date of the attack, I happened to be a student on another NOLS course, this one in Montana's Absaroka-Beartooth Wilderness. My mom heard about it on the local news that night, and I can only imagine her initial panic when she heard the phrases "NOLS course," "bear attack," and "student from Denver" leave the anchor's mouth.

Bear spray is essentially a very large can of pepper spray. It isn't lethal, just aggravating, and it doesn't require you to be a good shot. Deploy the spray at a charging bear, and you'll create an uncomfortable distraction between yourself and your would-be attacker, hopefully allowing you to safely leave the area.

If you bury bear spray in your backpack, you might as well not be carrying it at all, as the boys in the Talkeetnas learned that July night. When a bear starts charging, you don't have much time to deploy a defense mechanism. You should shoot your shot when a bear is 30 to 60 feet away; they can move up to 35 miles per hour if they're in a hurry. You do the math—it's not enough time to futz with zippers or think about where you've stashed something.

On my own NOLS course, more than 2,600 miles away but still very much in grizzly bear territory, each travel group of four students carried its own canister of bear spray as the course moved from one camp to the next. We'd been told not to put bear spray in our backpacks, and whomever had been designated the Carrier of the Spray that day had cleverly stuck the canister in a flimsy water bottle pocket on the side of their pack.

You can probably guess where this is going. At some point after scrambling through a boulder field just above an alpine lake, we realized the bear spray was gone. We had a decision to make: Should we retrace our steps through the boulder field or press on?

At the time, I'll admit, the argument for going back to look for the spray that I found most compelling was not wanting to explain to our instructors and the other students (we traveled in separate groups to minimize impact) that we'd lost our bear spray. I've always craved external validation, and this was no exception; I was going to be *good at backpacking*. It certainly wasn't the best reason to want to find it—a better reason would have been "We are traveling in grizzly bear country and I want to have an effective defense mechanism in the relatively likely event that we encounter a bear"—but the result is the same.

Fortunately, it had fallen out not long before our realization, and the detour added only about 20 minutes to our hike for the day. When we found the bright red canister, the culprit who'd very nearly lost it snatched it right up, running the sternum strap of their pack through the holster to ensure the spray was accessible and, just as importantly, not going anywhere.

Bear spray works most of the time. A 20-year study published in the *Journal of Wildlife Management* found that, in 83 incidents where bear spray was used, it worked to stop "undesirable behavior" 92 percent of the time on brown bears and 90 percent of the time on black bears. "Of all persons carrying sprays," the study's abstract notes, 98 percent "were uninjured by bears in close-range encounters." In a landscape where safety is never totally guaranteed, these strike me as pretty good odds.

I hear a lot of talk about the idea of carrying a gun in addition to or instead of bear spray. I'm not going to delve too deeply into the nuances of that argument and the comparative efficacy of guns versus bear spray. I am not a bear biologist. What I can tell you is this: More people are qualified to operate bear spray than have the training to safely carry and fire a gun. The consequences of incorrectly deploying bear spray (which, again, is very difficult to do, given the intentionally straightforward technique) are very different than those of accidentally or poorly shooting a firearm.

Another difference between the two deterrent methods is that while I want to stay safe in the backcountry, I don't *want* to kill a bear who's simply trying to make a living in its natural ecosystem for the sake of my own recreation—that doesn't feel ethical to me. My personal outlook? I'd rather make a lot of effort to avoid a bear and use my statistically 98 percent effective deterrent as a last resort.

Whatever you choose as your bear deterrent method, whether it's carrying bear spray or a firearm, a key factor is knowing how to use it. A gun is useless if you haven't practiced shooting it; bear spray is rendered ineffective if you don't know how to deploy it.

Even if you've done everything "right"—you're hiking in a group, avoiding terrain where you might surprise a bear, carrying bear spray within reach—you might still encounter a bear. This is a risk you must be willing to accept if you're traveling in a place where bears live.

When you deploy your bear spray, it might be carried off by the wind. It might blow back onto you. It might make a little fizzing sound and come trickling out of the nozzle instead of spraying, in which case you will have almost no time to wonder about the last time you checked the expiration date. It's also possible that a particularly determined individual will barrel right through your cloud of pepper spray and attack you anyway, which is why you should know what to do when a bear attacks you.

Let's pause briefly to talk about the difference between grizzly and black bears. It is a common misconception that all black bears are black and all grizzly bears are brown.* Black bears can be black, sure, but they can also be cinnamon-colored. Grizzly bears are

---

* Don't be thrown by the name "brown bear." These guys are the same species as grizzly bears, and though they're a different subspecies—all grizzly bears are brown bears, but not all brown bears are grizzly bears—this distinction matters only if you are a biologist and not at all if you are being attacked.

often a lighter brown, but they can also have very dark hair. And while grizzly bears as a species tend to be larger than black bears, size, too, can be an unreliable indicator—an adult male black bear (a boar) might be larger than a juvenile grizzly, for example. So, how to tell the difference?

If you are in a place where there are no grizzly bears, this is easy: Any bear you see is probably a black bear. (If this does not turn out to be the case, congratulations! You have made a discovery that is very important to bear research.)

If you are in grizzly bear habitat—Washington, Idaho, Montana, Wyoming, Alaska, much of western Canada—you should know a few things about bear identification. Grizzly bears, in addition to *generally* being larger and *generally* being lighter in color, have dished faces; short, rounded ears; and a large shoulder hump. Black bears have straighter noses; taller, pointier ears; and a distinct lack of shoulder hump. They are also very likely to run away when they see you.

The moment you spot a bear, take a minute to make some important observations. What kind of bear are you looking at? Is it alone, or are there cubs—or maybe an obvious food source? How far away is it? What's it doing—ignoring you and continuing to forage, or turning to face you, squaring up, clacking its teeth, making a snorting sound?

First things first: Do not run. When my dog sees a squirrel, he tenses up, ready to pounce. If it doesn't do anything, he'll lose interest. If it runs? All bets are off. Running triggers something in him, and his prey drive kicks in. He's going for it. Bears have this instinct, too. I mentioned earlier that they can run up to 35 miles per hour. Usain Bolt, the fastest human being on the planet, has clocked speeds of just under 28 miles per hour. You are not as fast as Usain Bolt, and even he cannot outrun a bear.

If it's a lone black bear you see, get loud. These are giant raccoons, remember? Make a lot of noise. Get big. Throw sticks and rocks. Yell: "GET OUT OF HERE, BEAR!" It probably will. Leave the area quickly (still no running), and do not climb a tree. Black bears are excellent climbers, and it has probably been a long time since you climbed a tree. You're far better off shuffling down the trail with your head on a swivel so you can keep an eye out.

If you're staring down a grizzly—or any bear with cubs, in which case the expression "don't get between a mama bear and her cubs" is very much a thing—stay calm and begin putting distance between yourself and the bear. (This applies whenever a bear is guarding something, be it a cub or a carcass.) Back away. Get ready to use your bear spray. Slowly and as if your life depends on it, because it very well might, unclip the spray from its holster and hold it out in front of you. Maybe the bear will lose interest and wander off, in which case you should leave the area quickly (but not at a run!). Stay alert.

If the bear charges, you don't have much time to think, so etch this into your neural pathways: When it's 10 to 20 yards away, deploy your bear spray. This should cause a charging bear some distress; it's got pepper spray in its eyes and ears and nostrils. Hopefully that works, and you can quickly (but not at a run!) leave the area.

Worst-case scenario: The bear spray doesn't work for one reason or another, and there's a bear attacking you. I'm not going to underplay it. This is bad. Keep your backpack on—this could help protect your back. Wait until the bear is truly upon you to drop to the ground and play dead. Protect your organs by lying on your stomach. Clasp your hands behind your neck, using your elbows to protect your face. Lie motionless and stay silent: You were a threat, and now you have been neutralized.

When you believe the bear has left, stay right where you are for a few minutes. If you've been attacked by a sow, she'll need time to collect her cubs. In any case, your attacker might still be watching for a moment, and if you get up too soon, you're back to being a threat. As soon as you're able to, collect yourself and get out of there. Don't run.

If all this sounds really, really awful, that's because it is. Make no mistake—your primary goal in bear country should be to avoid an encounter altogether. The odds of being attacked by a grizzly bear while hiking in, say, Yellowstone National Park are 1 in 232,613 person travel days. By following bear safety protocols, you can further ensure that your outing is a fun and uneventful one—and that you don't contribute to a bear's habituation.

LESSONS LEARNED

- **Store food properly.** The best way to avoid a bear encounter in camp is to store your food properly. Some frontcountry campsites also have "bear boxes," metal boxes with bear-proof locks. If those aren't available, Larson recommends storing food in a cooler in your car. In the backcountry, where this isn't an option, there are various methods for storing food. So-called bear hangs, which involve hanging one's food and other smelly objects (toothpaste, etc.) from a sturdy branch at least 12 feet off the ground, have largely fallen out of favor; backpackers often don't manage to hang their food sufficiently high or far enough from the trunk to keep bears from getting to it. "The main thing is you want to keep a bear out of your campsite," Larson says. "Would you rather have a bear just get at your food, or would you rather have him tear up all your gear to get at your food?" This means storing your food in a bear canister (available at most outdoor retailers) at least 150 yards from your campsite.

- **Know who you're up against.** While the principles of human-bear encounters are the same regardless of which species you're dealing with (avoid them, store your food properly, don't run or climb a tree), some basic bear identification skills will serve you well. In addition to understanding how to identify black versus grizzly bears, do some research to understand which species you're likely to encounter on your outing. Have there been any recent encounters? Are there areas or specific trails that are known for particularly heavy ursine traffic? Get a lay of the land before you head out, and you'll be able to more competently deal with a bear situation should one arise.

- **Plan your hike to avoid bears.** In general, bears do not strike randomly. Understanding when and where bears tend to be seen is a good way to avoid encountering one. They are most active at dawn, dusk, and night, so stick to established trails and steer clear of known bear habitat—willows, streambeds—during those times. Hiking alone is never without risk, and that risk increases when you're in bear country. Of the 44 people injured in grizzly encounters in Yellowstone National Park since the 1970s, 91 percent were traveling alone or with just one person. If you're traveling with just one other person, plan to talk or sing loudly as you're hiking. The bigger the group, the louder you'll be, and the more likely a bear is to hear you coming and skedaddle before there's a problem.

- **Be alert.** Bears have excellent senses of hearing and smell, but that doesn't guarantee they'll notice you first. They also have a lot going on, like foraging and generally going about their bear business, so you need to be hypervigilant in bear country. In addition to scanning your surroundings for an actual bear, you can watch out for bear tracks in the trail, markings on trees and poles, and bear scat. (Before you head out, it's worth spending some time studying up on photos of tracks, tree markings, and scat to give you a sense of what you're looking for.) You don't have to become an expert in tracking, but knowing how fresh a sign is gives you a sense of whether you can continue on your intended trajectory or need to leave the area.

- **Carry bear spray (and know how to use it).** If you're traveling in grizzly bear country, you need to carry bear spray. You can't fly with it, so if you're reaching your destination by plane, make arrangements to buy or rent some between landing at the airport and hitting the trail. Make sure the spray isn't expired. It absolutely must be on the outside of your pack (secured, as I learned in the Absaroka-Beartooths), preferably on your person and within easy reach. Some manufacturers sell bear spray along with a little holster; this gives you an extra handle to secure the canister to your pack but isn't strictly necessary. As I mentioned earlier in this chapter, bear spray is utterly ineffective if you don't know how to use it, so take the time to do a dry run before you head out into grizzly territory.

Chapter Three

Fourteen Thousand Feet

My first Fourteener was an easy one. Grays Peak—one of the 53 Colorado peaks whose summits are over 14,000 feet above sea level, known affectionately as "Fourteeners"—is just over 50 miles from Denver. It's alluring not only because it's a walk-up (in other words, there's an obvious trail the whole way to the top) but also because it shares a ridgeline with another Fourteener, Torreys Peak, making it a perfect two-for-one outing.

Despite that I'd grown up in Colorado, I was something of a late bloomer, Fourteener-wise. I didn't hike Grays until the summer I was 20. My best friend, Jordan, and I were taking summer classes, which meant we'd ride our bikes from our apartment in Superior to the University of Colorado campus in Boulder. We'd usually hit the gym at our apartment complex when we got home, too. (We were in incredible shape, and to this day I want to throttle my 20-year-old self for thinking I looked anything but phenomenal.)

At some point, things that used to feel hard—hiking the Royal Arch Trail from Chautauqua, racing up a flight of stairs with seconds to spare before a lecture started—didn't feel so hard anymore, and we were looking for a challenge. I can't remember which of us came up with the idea, but Jordan and I decided we'd hike a Fourteener.

We did a little research, mostly by Googling "Fourteeners to hike" and thumbing through a dusty early edition of Gerry Roach's *Colorado's Fourteeners*, which I'd swiped from my parents. We settled on Grays and Torreys for two primary reasons: We could afford the gas to get there from our apartment in a Boulder suburb, and the drive wasn't far enough to necessitate camping. This was key since neither of us owned any of the required gear, such as a tent. Besides, what better way to kick off what was sure to be an illustrious Fourteener career, we reasoned, than by knocking two off the list at once?

Reader, we did not knock two off our list at once.

We arrived at the trailhead in Jordan's rattletrap Subaru Outback sometime around 7:30 a.m.—early for a couple of college students who'd almost certainly been on the Hill until the wee hours the night before, but an insufficient alpine start by any other standard.

Blissfully unaware that we'd gotten an embarrassingly late start, we charged up the trail for approximately a quarter mile before we had to slow down.

"How high are we?" Jordan asked me.

"I dunno," I shrugged, gazing up the trail toward the summit, which now seemed impossibly far away. "Somewhere around 14,000 feet, I guess?"

The wooded trails near campus were at just over 6,000 feet, and we crushed out miles on them with no problem. Up here, though, things were already feeling a little different.

We resolved to take our time—we still had a long way to go.

The hike was largely uneventful, and I cannot emphasize enough how entirely this is due to good fortune. We took a couple of breaks, during which I pawed through my backpack (the same one I used to carry my books to class) for the half-liter water bottle I'd packed. When we reached the summit of Grays, hungry and fresh out of water, Jordan and I played chicken for a few minutes.

"So . . . where's the trail to get over to the other one?" she asked me.

My gaze panned around the windswept summit. "I mean, I could also totally just go back to the car, if you want," I said.

"Oh, good," she said, visibly relieved. "I thought for sure you were going to make us do this again." This had, in fact, been my intention. But by the time we made the summit, I was too exhausted to consider going up for even a few more feet before heading back down.

For our first Fourteener, we made decent time; we were back at the parking lot by early afternoon. (It's good to be 20.) As we dropped our packs and took off our shoes, Jordan turned to me seriously.

"I . . . don't think it's my goal to do all the Fourteeners," she said.

"God, me neither," I told her. With that, we piled back into her car and started discussing what kind of pizza we'd order down the hill in Idaho Springs.

Name a Fourteener in Colorado, and chances are someone's been injured or killed there. This isn't entirely because they're inherently dangerous. Peak bagging is a popular pastime in Colorado, which means the nontechnical Front Range Fourteeners—Bierstadt, Quandary, my old friends Grays and Torreys, and a few other neighbors—might see hundreds of ascents on a busy summer weekend. Even the ones requiring third-class scrambles and longer-distance hikes like Longs and Pikes Peaks see plenty of traffic, since they're relatively short distances from the Denver metro area.

The Colorado Fourteeners Initiative (CFI), a Golden-based nonprofit that organizes volunteer stewardship and trail maintenance projects and collects Fourteener data, estimated 353,000 hiker use days* on the state's highest peaks in 2018. CFI started

---

* A "hiker use day" or "person day" is one individual's ascent on a specific day. A hiker who visits Quandary Peak on three separate days would be counted three separate times; a single visitor who

counting Fourteener trail users with infrared cameras in 2014; the annual hiker day total has risen by more than 100,000 since that year. Bierstadt and Quandary Peaks typically vie for the number one spot, and CFI estimates that in 2018 they each saw between 35,000 and 40,000 hiker days.

But just because lots of people hike the "easy" ones doesn't mean there's no inherent risk—there absolutely is. These risks overlap with those of climbing just about any mountain, though they're compounded by the elevation, which puts hikers at risk of various altitude illnesses. And there's something alluring about that elevation—not just "I've climbed a mountain," but "I've climbed a *Fourteener*." People want that badge of honor, and sometimes they're beset with summit fever, unable to make good decisions when faced with the possibility of a prestigious summit.

The Fourteeners have another draw, which is that many climbers have set out to do them all. There are more than 50 peaks above 14,000 feet in Colorado—the exact number is often argued over; if you're less concerned with each summit having at least 300 feet of prominence from its nearest neighbors, you might count up to 58. I'm going with the number described in Roach's *Colorado's Fourteeners* guidebook: 53.

In any case, climbing them all is no small undertaking, and lots of hikers take decades to do it. By the time they get to the end of their list and the marathon is nearly over, the possibility of waiting another season to complete the list is pretty unappealing.

This was true for Mary Cronin, the first woman to climb all the Fourteeners. By the time she finished her list in 1934, she'd been working on it for 13 years. That last summer, she was on a mission: She summitted her last four peaks all in quick succession.

---

hikes Quandary, Bierstadt, and Evans would be counted each time. In other words, CFI does not estimate that 353,000 people hiked the Fourteeners in 2018, but rather that the Fourteeners were hiked 353,000 times.

Today, there are few firsts left for most Fourteener completers—they've been skied and hiked and climbed by all manner of routes, sometimes all in one season, so opportunities for first ascents require considerable creativity at this point. But that doesn't mean summit fever can't set in.

When my uncle, John Wullschleger, neared the end of his list in 2010—the same year Jordan and I set out to do Grays and Torreys—he'd been slowly collecting Fourteener summits for 40 years. He climbed his first Fourteener, Snowmass Mountain, on a Colorado Mountain Club outing in 1970, when he was 12 years old. Over the intervening decades, he racked up a summit here and there, but it wasn't his primary focus; he did stints as a car-less student and lived out of state for work. When he moved back to our home state for good in 2000, he decided he'd finally finish that list. ("Even then, it still took me another decade," he chuckles.)

John did his last six Fourteeners in 2010. He planned to do his last couple of peaks, the Wilson group, in one push via a ridge that connects the Wilson and El Diente summits. But when he got ready to start hiking at 5:00 a.m., the weather wasn't cooperating.

"It was pouring so hard I couldn't see the mountain," he remembers. He waited in his tent in the valley below until 2:00 that afternoon. When the clouds finally cleared, he made a break for the Wilson summit. (This isn't an optimal start time for newer hikers, but after 40 years and more than 50 summits above 14,000 feet, John had a good sense of how mountain weather works and how long the hike would take him.) Instead of tagging a second summit in the dark, he took an extra day to finish the list.

When the goal is tantalizingly close, it's hard to wait another day, let alone consider heading home and making yet another trip. But after four decades, there was no point in rushing it. John hiked to the top of his final Fourteener the next day, and thanks at least in part to his common sense, he's gone on to stand atop many more peaks since. This was a kind of level-headedness I hadn't yet acquired at age 20.

When I look back on the day Jordan and I climbed our first Fourteener, it's easy for me to see the headlines.

"Two CU Students Caught in Thunderstorm High on Grays Peak," the *Denver Post* might have reported. Or "Boulder Women Rescued on Grays."

We did a lot of things wrong that day, and it would have been easy for those errors to cascade—one bad decision leads to the next, whose consequences are compounded by the previous bad decision.

First, we got an inexcusably late start. In Colorado, where wild thunderstorms roll in like clockwork most summer afternoons, conventional wisdom suggests leaving the trailhead before dawn, which should allow the average hiker enough time to make the summit and be back below tree line by noon at the latest. Leaving at 7:30 a.m., long after the smarter hikers had gotten started, meant Jordan and I had way less time to make the summit, but we got lucky—this was a rare stormless day, and the weather stayed sunny all afternoon.

We didn't bring nearly enough water, and if we brought any snacks at all, I don't remember them. After most of a summer of training, though, our bodies were used to operating at a bit of a deficit, and we were in good enough shape to make it back to the car fairly quickly, a little parched rather than dangerously dehydrated.

We didn't carry a map or compass, assuming the trail would be obvious and we'd see plenty of other hikers, and we were right—we were never alone for long. But if we'd hit notorious I-70 traffic (frequently stop-and-go on a summer weekend morning, even back then) and started a little later and all the responsible hikers had already finished up for the day, or if a freak summer blizzard had rolled in and made it impossible to see the trail, we'd have been out of luck.

Speaking of unexpected weather, I don't think we carried any extra layers. I hiked in a tank top. I might have had a flimsy windbreaker stuffed in my backpack, but certainly nothing to insulate against the cold. I shudder to think what it would've been like if we'd lost the trail or been caught in a storm and had to spend the night out.

We had no first aid supplies, either. Honestly, I don't think it ever occurred to us. Fortunately, considering we'd have had no idea what to do with gauze or bandages or Steri-Strips (and had no spare water to clean out a wound), we didn't need them.

We finished the day eating pizza and sleeping in our own beds, rather than waiting for a rescue crew to arrive. If the intervening years have taught me one thing, it's that things shook out that way because we were lucky, not because we're in any way special. But not everyone gets so lucky.

In fact, Brad McQueen, his wife, Melissa, and his father, Rich, were way more prepared than Jordan and I when they set out to hike Mount Evans, another Front Range Fourteener, in 2001. At the time, Brad had completed 16 of the Fourteeners, eight of them (including a winter ascent) with his dad. Melissa was an avid hiker, too.

I met Brad when I was working as the office manager for a Denver-based trail stewardship nonprofit on whose board he served at the time. When we were introduced, someone mentioned offhand that Brad had climbed all the Fourteeners (not to mention dozens of other high peaks around the world). It wasn't until I was looking for some supply in the office basement and discovered a copy of Brad's book, *Exposed: Tragedy & Triumph in Mountain Climbing*, that I realized his illustrious mountaineering career had gotten off to a very rocky start.

At 14,264 feet, Mount Evans is the 14th-tallest summit in Colorado. Aside from its distinction as a Fourteener, its height isn't particularly notable; it doesn't boast an aesthetic skyline or an especially compelling route to the top. What it does have, though, is the highest paved road in North America. The 28-mile-long Mount Evans Scenic Byway gains 7,000 vertical feet on its journey from Idaho Springs to the summit of the peak.

Of all the people who stand on Evans's summit each year, the vast majority reach it by driving there. There's also a nice, short hike from Summit Lake, which Gerry Roach recommends "if you are more interested in an outing than a climb."

The McQueens planned to hike to the summit via the nine-mile West Ridge route. It begins at the Guanella Pass trailhead, the traditional starting point for neighboring Mount Bierstadt, and winds its way through a thick crop of willows. The relatively gentle Class 2 trail skirts the summit of 13,842-foot Mount Spalding, and here's where McQueen led his family off-route: Instead of following the trail to the right and traversing along the 13,200-foot contour line over to Mount Evans, the trio headed straight up to the Spalding summit.

It was a pretty small mistake, in the scheme of things. All three McQueens felt fine, it was still early in the day, and a late spring storm wasn't forecast to roll in until the following day. It was a bonus summit, really. They still had plenty of gas in the tank to tag the Evans summit and make it back to the trailhead.

To get from Spalding to Evans requires a southern descent of about 250 vertical feet to a saddle below, followed by a climb of 400 vertical feet up to Evans's northwest ridge, which is back on the route they'd intended to follow and would lead them to the summit.

But here's where McQueen made his second mistake: Instead of descending to the south, he led his wife and father down from the summit to the east, confusing 13,307-foot Mount Warren for his intended target.

"How I looked at a mountain 500 feet shorter than the one we were standing on and thought it was Mt. Evans, I just don't know," he writes in his book, adding that he "was clearly not thinking properly at 13,800 feet that day." It wasn't until they'd descended over 1,000 vertical feet and begun climbing the ridge to the Warren summit that the McQueens realized they were still off-route.

"I'm a firm believer that it's generally not the first bad decision you make that gets you into a bad situation," Brad told me over the phone as I researched this book. "It's the second, third, fourth decision you make. Recognize those critical decision points along the way, and question yourself—'Is this potentially bad decision number one? number two?' It's a good way to check yourself and make sure you don't get in over your head."

Brad's describing the commonly held idea that decisions in high-risk environments begin to compound, and that one bad decision can very often make way for another, and then another. The Swiss cheese model posits that the systems and processes we use to keep ourselves safe in high-risk fields (healthcare, aviation, and certainly in mountaineering) are like slices of Swiss cheese. The holes are weaknesses in those processes: a blind spot, a human error. The idea is to create checks and balances that prevent the holes from lining up with one another: You might make a mistake like getting off-route, in other words, but then you rectify it by retracing your steps or bagging the climb altogether to prevent errors from cascading. When we don't use those checks and balances, the errors begin to accumulate, and soon there's a big hole to fall through.

"Most people will get away with starting at 9:00 a.m., with wearing jeans, with not having enough water," Brad says. "But occasionally, those things will align, and all of a sudden, they become really important."

Instead of turning around and heading back the way they came, the McQueens spotted the Mount Evans Road and descended to Mile 23, then walked five miles from there to the summit. By the time they arrived, they'd hiked 9.5 miles—0.6 miles farther than the entire roundtrip hike was supposed to be.

While they'd been hiking, the family's view to the west—the direction from which Rocky Mountain weather typically rolls in— had been obscured. Now, though, they could see what was headed their way, and it didn't look good.

As the McQueen family began descending the West Ridge toward Guanella Pass, snow started to fall. Soon, it made the route's broken slabs and talus dangerously slippery. After hours of stumbling and postholing, made worse by accumulating snow, they managed to make it below tree line, although tree line is a generous description for the dreaded willows that make up the meadow below Mount Bierstadt. It took them another hour and a half to push through the four- to six-foot willows, during which time Melissa and Rich both fell through a collapsed snow bridge into a creek.

Eventually, the trio found a stand of trees and hunkered down at 11,500 feet. It was a long, cold night, especially for the two who'd gotten wet. Fortunately, all three of them (and their golden retriever, Malcolm, who'd accompanied them on the hike) were alive the next morning when rescue crews—whom Brad's mother had alerted to the missing party—arrived at the trailhead.

The McQueens got lucky on Mount Evans, but not without consequence. Melissa's feet were badly frostbitten, and she spent 10 days in the hospital. Eventually, all but two of Melissa's toes had to be amputated. And that's to say nothing of the trauma associated with such a close call. (Brad says the experience of writing *Exposed* was cathartic, and he thinks about the accident far less frequently than he did before he wrote the book.)

"We made a good decision to stay together," he told me. Brad is frank about what it might have meant to split up that night: "If we had separated, I think Melissa or my dad may not have survived the night."

There are exceptions, of course—emergencies, mostly, wherein one person absolutely needs to go for help—but splitting up is almost never a good idea.

One of the highest-profile examples of the danger of separating from one's party is the tragic 2005 disappearance of Michelle Vanek on 14,005-foot Mount of the Holy Cross. This was big news in my home state, where I'd just started my sophomore year of high school. I remember my parents, casual hikers who'd both grown up in Colorado, reading about it in the *Denver Post*.

Vanek was hiking with a friend who'd hiked 37 of the Fourteeners at the time of this outing—he was a fairly experienced peak bagger. Vanek, on the other hand, was hiking her first-ever Fourteener.

It's easy to be lulled into complacency by a peak that's close to home, particularly if it's considered "easy." Holy Cross, as it's often called, is just two and a half hours from Denver. It's not technically demanding—there's a trail all the way to the top—but Fourteeners, as I learned on my Grays Peak hike and on every one I've climbed since, are never *easy*. This one in particular requires a hike up and over Half Moon Pass, followed by a descent, before the climb to the summit begins in earnest.

In fact, Vanek and her companion began encountering problems before they even really started. Because she was inexperienced, Vanek trusted her friend to make all the decisions about their climb. But despite having ticked plenty of other peaks off his list, he wasn't a professional guide and didn't have significant experience leading or instructing novice climbers. He didn't know that two separate trails leave from the Half Moon Pass parking lot, and instead of starting up the standard route to the summit, he led Vanek up the Fall Creek Trail. He didn't realize his error until they'd hiked for an hour.

At that point, Vanek's companion also realized he'd left his water filter and his lunch in the car. He had a copy of a map from a guidebook, meant for illustrative purposes only, but no topo map or compass for navigation. But instead of turning around to start up the correct trail or bagging the hike altogether, he consulted his photocopied map and saw another route to the summit. It was the Halo Route, a significantly longer and harder route—but one that wouldn't require them to backtrack. The *Vail Daily* would later report that local hikers were surprised to hear of a first-time Four-teener hiker taking what it called an "unconventional, circuitous and partially unmarked route to the top."

"It seemed like a good idea given their situation," writes Mark Scott-Nash in his *Colorado 14er Disasters,* "except for one thing: They had been making one mistake after another. Their cascade of errors was growing."

Soon, the 2,000-foot climb up the harder route intensified, and Vanek's pace slowed. Scott-Nash speculates that she was probably suffering from acute mountain sickness, or AMS, given that the elevation of her home was between 5,000 and 6,000 feet and she was now nearing 13,000 feet above sea level. Vanek and her partner continued up and over Points 13,373 and 13,831, eventually stopping just a few hundred feet short of the Holy Cross summit proper.

Here, Vanek finished the last of her water and told her friend she was too tired to continue. (Understandable—what a day she'd already had, summiting two points over 13,000 feet!) He remem-bers that she told him to go on without her; the state's cold case file reports:

> Near the summit of Mt. Holy Cross, Michelle stated she was very tired and her friend told her to wait and he would go to the top and be right back. The friend stated he advised Michelle if she wanted to head back down, to follow the trail and he would catch up with her.

Not wanting to follow the same circuitous route back to the trailhead—this would be much less convenient than making a big loop—Vanek's friend suggested she stay on the same contour line. This way, Vanek would neither gain nor lose any elevation as she traversed below the summit from the saddle where they now sat over to the North Ridge Trail, the standard Holy Cross descent trail. The unmarked traverse would entail a mile-long off-trail scramble through an immense, unmarked boulder field.

When Vanek and her companion separated a little before 1:30 that afternoon, he didn't know it was the last time anyone would see her. But it was: Vanek wasn't at their agreed-upon meetup spot, nor was she waiting in the valley below Half Moon Pass or back at the car. More than 800 searchers and five helicopters would eventually put in 10,000 search hours—the largest search and rescue effort in Colorado history at that point—over the course of seven days, but no trace of Vanek has ever been found.

The Monday morning quarterback routine is a tempting one. From our comfortable living rooms, it's easy to read the facts about the events leading to Michelle Vanek's disappearance and wax poetic about all the things we'd have done differently.

But the truth is, I've made almost all the mistakes Vanek and her partner made that day. I've forgotten something in the car and decided not to go back for it. I've made wrong turns on the trail, scrambled across instead of going up and over, and brought friends for what I thought would be mellow hikes but which turned out to be way over their heads. In fact, I'd argue, most experienced hikers have probably made these mistakes—that's how we gain experience. If you don't see any of yourself in that ill-fated 2005 hike, either you're not being very self-critical or perhaps you're still relatively new to peak bagging and haven't had the time to make your own mistakes.

And as Brad McQueen points out, you're not thinking nearly as clearly at say, 13,800 feet above sea level as you are at your home in Denver. Especially if you've been there for a couple of hours.

Acute mountain sickness often presents as shortness of breath and fatigue. If you've ever driven over a high mountain pass and felt lightheaded or suffered a headache after a few hours at altitude, you've experienced it yourself. Eventually, AMS sufferers might begin to look or act as if they're drunk; wilderness medicine practitioners call this phenomenon the "umbles"—mumbles, bumbles, stumbles. Left unchecked, AMS can progress quickly to high-altitude cerebral edema (HACE), a swelling of the brain, or its counterpart in the lungs, high-altitude pulmonary edema (HAPE). Both are life-threatening.

There's an old adage in wilderness medicine that there are three treatment options for AMS: descend, descend, descend. Cute. But, really, the only way to knock symptoms of AMS is to get to a lower elevation. Sometimes, on peaks higher and more technical than the Colorado Fourteeners (and, in fact, even on the Fourteeners and at lower elevations), this necessitates a rescue. But if you pay close attention to how you're feeling and turn around before it becomes an emergency, it's possible to make it back down to the trailhead under one's own power with mild or moderate symptoms of AMS.

I didn't experience altitude sickness myself (at least, not in a way that really affected me) until years after Jordan and I hiked Grays Peak. Frankly, having grown up at nearly 6,000 feet above sea level, I always figured altitude sickness was something that happened to people from the plains and coasts, not to Coloradans.

Longs Peak is visible from just about anywhere in the Front Range. Its sheer east face, the Diamond, cuts a striking silhouette on the skyline from Denver or Boulder. I first climbed it right after college. My then-boyfriend and I got a coveted permit to camp in Goblins Forest. We spent a damp night there, then hiked to the summit via the third-class Keyhole Route. Gerry Roach describes hiking this route on a late summer weekend as "like walking on a crowded city sidewalk in a construction zone"; despite the crowds, Roach adds that it's "a long, arduous ascent on a high, real mountain."

We hiked in the predawn darkness to the base of the Boulder Field, at the top of which sits the route's namesake feature. The Keyhole, a notch on the rocky ridge that connects Longs Peak with its neighbor, Storm Peak, was slowly illuminated as the sun rose behind us. From the Keyhole, hikers follow red-and-yellow bulls-eyes painted on the rocks to stay on-route through aptly named sections of the route like the Trough, the Narrows, and the Home-stretch. It's a steep scramble, spooky in wet weather; lucky for us, the weather was perfect the day we climbed the Keyhole route.

When we summited around midmorning, we snapped a few photos but didn't linger—the roundtrip climb from our campsite to the summit and back to the trailhead would add up to a little less than 13.5 miles, so we still had a long day ahead. I felt tired, having started the hike hours before my usual wake-up time, but otherwise fine.

By the time we got back to our tent, though, I noticed that my knuckles were all swollen. It looked like I had puffy, oversized Mickey Mouse hands poking out from my windbreaker. This, I would later learn, is a common side effect of an electrolyte imbal-ance; I was dehydrated after our big climb, which was probably exacerbated by the elevation. We stopped at a gas station in Estes Park to grab some Gatorade, and later that evening, I felt fine. (I think I even went to a friend's birthday party at a bar in Denver—oh, to have the boundless energy of my 21-year-old self!)

So when I set out to climb Longs via the Cables route with Bix a few years later, I remembered my cartoon hands and carried more water than I thought I'd need. I'd learned the basics of Fourteener climbing over the interceding handful of years. Knowing the hike to the base of the technical climb would take us two or three hours, we left the trailhead around 3:30 a.m. We made good time to the turnoff for Chasm Lake, where the more difficult Diamond routes begin, and continued to follow the standard trail to the Keyhole.

The approach to the Cables route, named for a series of steel cables that used to occupy Longs's North Face, is the same as that of the Keyhole as far as the Boulder Field, where some parties camp overnight for an early start the next morning. They eyebolts that held them in place remained when the cables were removed in 1973, and to this day, they're often used as belay and rappel anchors. A couple of pitches of 5.3 climbing up west-facing slabs and corners, a scramble up some broken ledges to the southeast, and you're at the summit. From there, you can descend via the Keyhole route or rappel back down to the Boulder Field via the same route.

As we neared the Boulder Field that morning, I started to feel off. My hands were a little swollen, which I already knew wasn't unusual for me. But there was something else. Despite that I was very fit—and that I'd felt great when we started hiking that morning—I started to lag behind Bix.

I began to feel a dull ache behind my eyes. Half an hour later, as the Boulder Field came into view and the sun was just starting to make an appearance on the eastern horizon, my headache had evolved from dull to splitting.

We'd agreed to stop, organize our climbing gear, and wait for sunup at the Boulder Field. When I got there, my vision shaky from my headache, Bix was perched on a boulder watching the sunrise. I dropped my pack and slumped to the ground, murmuring something about my headache. This was not how I'd envisioned the climb going—Bix and I had been dating for only a few months, and I wanted very much to seem tough and capable. I also, at 23, felt that my worth was closely tied to whatever difficult accomplishment I'd made the previous weekend, and hiking to the base of a climb, only to turn around without making the summit, did not qualify.

This is not unusual, and there's relatively little scientific understanding of when and why altitude illness strikes. It can happen to the fittest climbers, or it can happen once at 12,000 feet and then never materialize the following weekend at 14,000. It is, in other words, not necessarily tied to one's training or fitness, let alone to one's worth as a human being.

Perhaps fortunately, I didn't have the wherewithal to do anything reckless. After 15 minutes of closing my eyes and hoping my headache would dissipate, it progressed instead to throbbing, and I knew there was no way I could keep moving, let alone safely place gear, manage a rope, or belay my boyfriend. The climb was off.

Of course, there's no way to know what would have happened if I hadn't thrown in the towel and slogged back to the trailhead. Everything might have been fine, although the conventional wisdom (treat altitude illness by descending) suggests otherwise. But a million little things, followed by a million others, might have happened: The holes in that day's slices of Swiss cheese might have aligned until there was no going back. In any case, I would have had a miserable time, and I am not a serious enough alpinist for this to be a point of pride.

I was disappointed not to make the climb, but that feeling lasted only a few days. I think about that day often, especially when I hear about an accident up high. That old proverb comes to mind: *There but for the grace of God go I.* Whatever you believe in, whether it's divine intervention or pure coincidence, it's a compelling reminder—that *could've* been you, and very often, it only *wasn't* you because of some small thing that happened to go right.

Now, thanks more to good luck than common sense (and the lessons learned on more than one failed summit attempt), I have many more summits to climb. Most importantly, thanks to what I know now, I'll probably abandon plenty more climbs—and live to tell about them.

LESSONS LEARNED
- **Pack the 10 Essentials.** I'm hard-pressed to think of a dire situation in the mountains that wouldn't be improved even slightly by having the 10 Essentials on hand. This list of items

was originally compiled in the 1930s by the Seattle-based Mountaineers climbing club. It's evolved since then, obviously, but the principle remains the same: If you need one of these items, you *really* need it. The 10 Essentials are navigation (map and compass, plus a GPS if you like), a headlamp, sun protection, first aid, a knife, a way to start a fire, shelter (this might be as simple as a lightweight space blanket), and extra food, water, and clothing. It might sound like a long list, but most of these items are small and lightweight, and having them all could very realistically save your life. If their combined weight seems like too much to carry up a Fourteener, that's probably an indication to train a bit more at lower elevations until you're comfortable with them on your back. Brad McQueen's father might well still have all his toes because of the extra socks Brad carried; I shudder to think how my first Fourteener outing might have ended if my packing (or, more accurately, lack thereof) had been put to the test.

- **Get an early start.** General hiking and mountaineering wisdom posit that it makes sense to start climbing hours before sunup. The alpine start's roots are in climbing high, snowy peaks, where reaching the summit and then descending before the sun warms the snow means you're less likely to encounter rockfall. By the time we're driving up from the Front Range in droves, the snow has largely released even the higher summits from its grips, so this is less of an issue. But the alpine start remains a crucial component of Fourteener bagging: Afternoon thunderstorms roll in like clockwork most days in the high country, and if you're above tree line when lightning strikes, you are very likely the tallest object around. As Brad McQueen points out, lots of people will get away with starting late—Jordan and I certainly did.

But why risk it? Even if the skies are clear and a rainless forecast holds true, you've still built a solid habit and given yourself more time to finish your climb.

- **Make your own decisions.** A tendency exists for very inexperienced climbers to blindly follow their more experienced counterparts' instructions. In avalanche decision-making, this heuristic trap is known as the "Expert Halo," wherein an informal leader ends up making crucial decisions for the group. Problematically, this leader is often just the person with the most experience (or the most willingness to speak up!). But "more experience than anyone else in the group" doesn't necessarily equate to "requisite experience to make safe decisions for the entire party." Michelle Vanek's companion had climbed 37 Fourteeners, but that didn't mean he had the training to guide a novice hiker. Knowing how to do something and being able to teach someone else to do it are two very different things—perhaps you had a high school teacher who knew their subject well, but couldn't quite find a way to convey it to their students. Sufficient experience to do something on one's own is not a substitute for being able to guide or teach novices. If you are climbing with someone more experienced than you, don't assume they know everything. Ask to be part of the decision-making process; try to understand *why* they're making those decisions. When you actively participate in your own risk management, you not only have an opportunity to avoid costly mistakes, you're also gaining important experience.

- **Turn around *before* it's an emergency.** Don't wait until it's too late to turn around. Don't wait until someone can't feel their toes or your headache is so bad you can't see or the clouds have darkened and you can feel their electricity on the back of your neck. By the time these things are happening, you are in the midst of an emergency, and your odds of making it off the mountain before utter catastrophe strikes have greatly diminished. View each decision as a point of no return, because that's what it is. If you go on with wet feet, you cannot undo your choice not to bring socks when a blizzard rolls in. If you forget a headlamp, you cannot un-forget it in the car when the trail stops looking familiar and the sun has started to set. These seemingly tiny things—things that didn't seem like a big deal in the morning, when you were fresh and eager to hit the trail—cascade until you cannot stop yourself from going over the waterfall. Remember that if you turn around before it's an emergency, you will have another chance to climb to the summit. Make it your mantra: *The mountain will be here next weekend. Will I?*

- **Stick together.** Despite what he now views as a cascade of errors, Brad and his family did a few things right on their Evans ordeal. Perhaps the most important decision they made that day was to not split up. There's more discussion of this principle in chapter 8, but it's critical enough that it bears repeating: Finish your climb with the people you started it with. Make no mistake—this means you might not summit. You can mitigate those odds by climbing only with people you trust or by having a very frank conversation about your goals before you set out. But in a dynamic environment filled with objective hazards, any of us might be laid low by altitude sickness, fatigue, or some other X factor. Part of partnership is being prepared to put our own goals on hold for the sake of someone else's best interest. Spare yourself the panic of returning to your meetup spot, only to have it slowly dawn on you that you may never see your partner alive again. No summit is worth this!

Chapter Four

Throw Bags and Throw Up

It's an uncharacteristically rainy May afternoon in Colorado, and I'm gasping for breath in the deep end of the Evergreen Rec Center pool.

What the hell am I doing here? I wonder, but I don't have much time to rethink my life choices.

"Again!" the head boatman cries, and I do my best to hoist my slippery carcass onto the upside-down raft for what feels like the hundredth time. I wedge the T-grip of my paddle into one of the boat's self-bailing holes, shakily rise to my feet, and flip the beast onto its back.

It is my first day of raft guide training, and right now, I'm pretty sure it will be my last.

Finally, our time is up and the Evergreen High School swim team starts trickling into the steamy pool. I'm relieved to see that the rest of the rookie class looks just as haggard as I feel, a fact I use to comfort myself as I stagger into the locker room to stare blankly at the wall and fight back tears until it's time to go.

The drive back to the shop in Idaho Springs is quiet, and I wonder whether any of the other rookies are feeling this discouraged.

We pull onto the I-70 frontage road and a trio of blue rubber rafts slides past us on Clear Creek. The guides wave heartily at our van, then turn back to their boats and steer effortlessly away from a partially submerged boulder, one of the creek's many obstacles. How do they make it look so easy?

Clear Creek, like the training its guides endure, is relatively short but very intense. It runs 66 miles to its output into the South Platte but contains some of the most continuous whitewater in Colorado, certainly on the Front Range. It holds the distinction of being the only creek in the United States fed by a river. This sounds glamorous, but let me assure you: It may be a wild ride, but it's not wilderness. The creek runs along I-70 for its typical "beginner" and "intermediate" runs, and along Highway 6 for the gnarlier canyon run. The only reason you can't hear the highway traffic is that it's overpowered by the roar of whitewater.

Guide trainings on other rivers teach their rookies how to look for and avoid undercuts and keeper holes, but on Clear Creek, we have rebar and old cars. The best line to run a given rapid might change overnight due to blasting along I-70, and existing obstacles are made easier to see by the presence of orange road cones and speed limit signs that have fallen into the creek, where it's too dangerous to try and retrieve them.

An enchanting trip into the wilderness it is not, but if you can guide Clear Creek, you can guide just about anywhere.

This was one of the many things that appealed to me about guiding the creek: I pictured myself guiding friends on long wilderness trips, gracefully piloting the boat down one rapid after the next as we made our way downriver, pulling over only for hot springs and beer breaks.

These were the raft trips my fantasies were made of—photos from my uncle's days of guiding on the Colorado, where everyone's smiling and looks young and tan and healthy; Kenton Grua's speed run through the Grand Canyon in a wooden dory; childhood memories of family vacations where we all donned matching personal flotation devices (PFDs) and arrived safely downstream with a handsome 20-year-old at the helm—excitement! Beautiful scenery! A general sense of safety and well-being!

My childhood friend Hannah's parents ran a raft guiding outfit when we were in grade school, and every summer, they'd let her invite our crew of friends out for a weekend trip. As we got older, her dad would take us to run the Arkansas River through Browns Canyon, just outside Buena Vista, Colorado.

Hannah's friends would be sorted into one of the family's mismatched set of boats, guided by a rotating cast of the young men her father employed. A few of them were somewhat maladjusted, all drank the kind of watery swill beer you'd expect from a twentysomething living in a tent in the Colorado mountains, and each put in his time guiding his employer's kids and their friends down the river.

It felt almost unimaginably grown-up to be floating the Arkansas with the only parents in sight a few boats ahead of us. For the guides, I imagine this felt a little less fun and a little more risky, considering what the Arkansas is capable of.

There have been more than 60 fatalities on the Arkansas, according to American Whitewater's accident database.* The year I learned to guide, an 11-year-old boy was thrown from his commercially guided boat in Brown's Canyon on what his family thought would be a day of splashy fun on the river.

Searchers found Drake Durkee's body three days later, hung up on a group of submerged rocks just a few feet from shore. The little boy whose elementary school principal described him as "a kind soul," who sang in the choir and inspired his friends to push themselves to a basketball championship, had just finished the fifth grade. In the days between his disappearance from the raft and the

---

* American Whitewater, a nonprofit river conservation organization, keeps a database of whitewater fatalities and close calls. A 1975 drowning at a slalom race incited swiftwater safety expert Charlie Walbridge to write up a report on foot entrapment, and since then, the database has cataloged more than 1,600 incidents dating back to 1972.

moment searchers found his body, his parents hiked up and down the railroad tracks along the river; his mother felt sick at the sound of the current.

Drake fell out of his boat in Big Drop Rapid, a Class III section. His empty PFD turned up shortly thereafter. He was such a fan of the Denver Broncos that his family buried him in a #88 jersey, a nod to his favorite player, Demaryius Thomas. They also started a foundation in his name and installed a "buddy bench" on his school's playground, where other kids can honor the exceptionally kind little boy's memory by taking a seat when they need a friend to talk to.

I have read hundreds of stories of accidents in the outdoors. All are sad, but there's something so wrenching about this one. Drake Durkee's death makes me feel choked up every time I think about it. Maybe it's because he's from my own hometown, or because I was around Drake's age when I started rafting the Arkansas. Or because the thought of a parent having to bury their sweet 11-year-old is unfathomable.

There's another factor, too. Throughout my career, I've taken my role as an outdoor professional really seriously. It weighs on me that when I am the guide, whether it's on easy trails near town or on whitewater, someone has put their safety and possibly even their very life in my hands. They've essentially said, "I don't know how to do this thing safely on my own," and I've accepted that responsibility. This family entrusted their kids to an outfitter, and one of them did not make it home alive. I've always known abstractly that that's a possibility, and this accident reminds me that it's not just theoretical.

In Colorado, commercial rafting is a $163 million industry. There is some regulation at the state level. As of this writing, rafting outfitters must pay a fee to register with the state, agree to inspections ensuring that they carry standard safety gear, and employ guides who meet the state's qualification standards. But a lot of things aren't regulated. There's no law about how old a kid has to be to go on raft trips billed as "intermediate" or "advanced," and no age limits related to periods of high water flows.

That's one of many reasons it's crucial to choose a reputable outfitter. The company that took Drake, his brother, and his grandpa rafting in Brown's Canyon advertised itself as having experienced guides and using the best safety equipment. In actuality, the *Denver Post* reports, the outfitter "was on its second summer of probation for violating state regulations," including multiple citations for failing to maintain records of its guides' qualifications and running trips without the required trip leaders, "and had been warned it could lose its permit unless it improved."

I want to be clear here that Drake's family is in no way at fault for assuming the company was as advertised. "It took the *Denver Post* multiple days, a Colorado Open Records Act request and more than $100 to receive a list of rafting companies on probation," that same report says. Most average citizens do not have the knowledge and resources of an investigative journalist. Now that you are armed with this information, I hope you'll research outfitters carefully before giving them your money and, more important, trusting them with your life. There's more detail on what to look for in the Lessons Learned section of this chapter.

Things came full circle in my teenage years, when Rio Expeditions had long since disbanded and the only evidence of its existence was the handful of boats Hannah's dad kept around for personal trips. In those halcyon days of my late teens and early 20s, my longtime friends and I enjoyed relative solitude and independence on an annual rafting trip to a meandering stretch of the Upper Colorado River. The run from the put-in at Pumphouse to one of the downstream take-outs at Radium, Rancho del Rio, or State Bridge is mellow enough that people regularly run it on stand-up paddleboards. A couple of Class III rapids require attention, especially at high flows, but for the most part, the fun-to-consequence ratio is good.

With three-two beer (the watered down kind available at Colorado gas stations at the time) purchased for us by older siblings, we set up camp at the put-in each summer, letting ourselves feel extra cool as we lazily floated by commercial boats full of Griswolds. The closest we came to scouting rapids was a map drawn by Hannah's dad on a cocktail napkin, admonishing us with a sad face and several exclamation points to avoid a certain exposed rock.

Pretty quickly after we'd all finished college, everyone stopped coming home for the summer, and the yearly pilgrimage to the Upper C petered out. Still, I managed not to let go of that feeling: the ineffable satisfaction of floating downstream, and the unique exhaustion of a day spent on the water.

It was with all this in mind that I signed up to learn to be a raft guide. I'd just finished graduate school and, determined to take a summer off from thinking about academics, I sent an application to an outfit whose boats I'd seen go by as we climbed in Clear Creek Canyon the previous summer.

I showed up to that first day of training with a nauseous feeling in the pit of my stomach and a light drizzle in the air, and things didn't exactly improve—in terms of the weather or my constitution—as the day dragged on. Nine hours later, I called my mom on the way home and cried.

There was absolutely no way, I told her, that I was going to make it through training. I think she was probably relieved, but it didn't last long.

I wish I could insert a Rocky Balboa–style montage here, alternating shots of me swimming fearlessly across the river, easily lifting boats above my head, and steering crews of customers around Clear Creek's myriad obstructions. I wish I could say I showed up on day two with renewed determination and nailed every drill, and that I knew right away that (a) this was my calling or (b) I never wanted to set foot in an inflatable rubber raft again.

But, as with most things, my progress was incremental. On the second day of training, we covered knots and rigging, and for one blissful hour I was back in my element. Figure eight, Muenter, double fisherman's, prusik, three-to-one: I knew them all, no problem.

In fact, water itself was the primary complication on my journey to become a raft guide: I was (and remain) terrified of it.

As long as I'm listing my neuroses, I should explain: I've always been quick to vomit. I'll puke because I'm nervous, excited, upset—any strong emotion, really.

Without even really being pressed, my mother likes to share this story from my childhood: When I was six, my parents took me to Disneyland, where I threw up every single morning. One morning, we were standing in line for Space Mountain, and I ralphed my chocolate chip Mickey Mouse–shaped pancakes all over myself—from excitement, she maintains—and she cleaned me up a little and sat me down on the ride. She probably got a few looks, but when you're stuck with a kid who can't keep their breakfast down, you get used to sidestepping a little vomit here and there.

All this brings up the inevitable question of why I thought it was a good idea to become a raft guide when the thought of swimming in whitewater literally makes me want to upchuck. The closest thing I have to an answer is this: If an anxious person like me never did anything I was afraid of, I'd never do anything at all.

So, in addition to being one of the most physically taxing two-week periods of my life—this includes weeks spent in the Alaskan interior in winter and a stint on the Harding Icefield with an 85-pound pack—guide training was an emotional drain, too.

At the end of that first week of training, the senior guides brought us to my old stomping grounds, the Upper Colorado. We put in at Pumphouse, just like my friends and I used to, only this time it was lightly snowing and I was wearing two wetsuits. Eventually, as it always does in Colorado, it warmed up enough for us to swim, an idea I'd been dreading to the point of nausea for the last six days.

One by one, the rookies swam across the wide, slow-moving river, which, even doubly wetsuited, was cold enough to briefly render me breathless. A few too-short seconds later, I was swimming back across, panic rising in my throat as the gentle current pushed me farther downstream from the boat. I steeled myself, and a little voice in my head reminded me to adjust my ferry angle. What felt like hours but was probably less than a minute later, I arrived at my destination only slightly worse for wear.

A hundred yards downstream from the spot where we lapped across the river sits a slick, green tongue of smooth water. This leads to a wave train, the entrance to a mellow Class II rapid known as Warm Up Rapid. The head boatman barked that we would each swim into the current, flip over into whitewater swim position (something akin to a starfish, heading feetfirst into the melee) through the wave train, and exit into an eddy on the opposite side of the river. He said all this as if it were perfectly normal, which caused the contents of my stomach to churn.

I waited until the other rookies were lined up on the shore and quietly informed him that there was absolutely no way in hell I could do that.

"I don't think I want to be a raft guide after all," I told him, barely holding back tears of dread.

Realizing that my fear was genuine, he softened a little. This particular boatman was a handsome, confident thirtysomething with enough seasons under his belt to think this rapid—this entire run, probably—was runnable in an innertube. His icy blue eyes made it clear, whenever an opportunity presented itself, that he had absolutely zero tolerance for bullshit of any kind. Eventually, perhaps because I am very charming but more likely because it's hard to be angry when someone is sincerely terrified, he offered to swim the rapid with me.

"Ethically," he told me gently, probably hoping not to be thrown up on, "you have to be willing to swim anything you'd take a client down."

Against my better judgment, I agreed. It was not the most dignified moment of my life, being swum across the river with a guide holding on to my life jacket. But seconds later, there I was, on the other side of the river, vomiting into the current.

As my rookie training progressed, spring began to look more like summer. Back at the shop in Idaho Springs, the snow stopped falling and started melting, water levels rose, and boats full of trainees were no longer the only ones on the river. We'd arrive at the put-in and wait for two or three other companies to load their clients into boats, give them a quick spiel on how to paddle, and get onto the creek.

A couple of weeks into the season, the boat I was in flipped at the top of a Class IV rapid in Clear Creek Canyon, spilling its contents—a guide, three rookies, and two customers—into the current. Double Knife looks as sinister as its name implies. Guides have to steer the boat to the left of a sharp, protruding rock, then immediately swing around to the right to avoid crashing into the canyon wall. It's a move that requires both power and precision; a small misstep can end in disaster.

The consequences of a flip in Double Knife are compounded by the fact that there's another Class IV rapid, Hells Corner, just downstream. A flip here means the guide has to get to the boat, flip it back over, and gather all the passengers in just a few hundred yards, or else everyone's going for a rough (and potentially fatal) swim.

At this point, I'd been through the rapid enough times to know exactly what should happen. But as we rounded the corner into

Double Knife, something felt off. *Oh*, it registered in my brain, *we're going to flip.*

Before I had time to think about what to do, I was under the boat, fighting my way to the surface. I struggled to keep my head above water as I pinballed between rocks. The current carried me past the boat, which the more experienced guide had already managed to right. He was working to pull the two customers into the boat and I realized, in a panic, that my only option was to swim for the opposite shore.

I'm not an especially strong swimmer, but if you'd seen me in that moment, I could have fooled you. It's funny what our bodies are capable of when their only other option is to literally die. As I neared the river's edge, I began clawing at the shore; the current was moving too quickly down the narrow corridor for me to catch one of the creek's notoriously tiny eddies. Finally, I pulled my way into the lee behind a boulder, giving me just enough of a break from the current to haul myself ashore, where I promptly puked into the dirt.

The same thing happened again the next day on a commercial trip run by a different company. This time, a passenger died.

The canyon was shut down for a few hours so rescue crews could recover her body. We were training just upstream at the time. The head boatman had my rookie class carrying boats around on the beach—"Now set it here," "Now put this one there"—to keep us occupied, but eventually someone overheard some radio chatter.

Initially, the talk was clinical: "A 47-year-old female has been pulled from the water. Efforts to resuscitate her are in progress."

Then the rumors started to swirl—a guide with another outfit heard this, someone else told one of our drivers that. The woman was visiting from Texas with her daughter. She was over the weight limit the company's life jackets could support, but instead of declining to put her on the boat or suggesting another trip or stocking their shelves with life jackets that would fit her, the company had shuttled her to the put-in and launched her boat into the water.

The boat had flipped in Double Knife (this I could picture with nauseating accuracy) and the guide hadn't been able to pull her back into the boat. He tried more than once, someone told me. The trip had been run with a safety kayaker—someone assigned to follow a commercial trip in a kayak in case of incidents like this one. He'd eventually managed to pull her to shore, where she was soon pronounced dead.

People were saying her daughter was still in the boat, that she'd seen the whole thing.

At that moment, I wanted to be anywhere else in the world. I'd have given anything to be sitting on my couch watching TV. Why hadn't I taken up tennis or knitting? Why was I standing in a wetsuit and holding a paddle two miles upstream from where a woman had just died—where I'd very nearly met my own end the day before?

But what could I do? The only way to get to the bus, back to the shop, back to my car, back home, was to get in a boat and run Double Knife. It did not help that, in my mid-20s, I was very invested in appearing to be much tougher than I was, particularly in front of a crew of macho guys. Our shared language was a salty one, peppered with affectionate insults. My greatest goal—after staying alive, but it was close—was to hide the fact that beneath all the bravado, I was scared out of my mind.

When my boat arrived near the entrance to the rapid, the head boatman announced nonchalantly that I would be the one to guide it.

"You've got to be kidding," I said, though I already knew that he was not. "No way!"

I had grown to trust him implicitly, but this was too much. He shrugged, gestured to his place at the back of the boat, and pulled his paddle out of the water. It was me piloting the boat or no one.

I couldn't let myself think too much about it—about that feeling yesterday of reaching the point of no return, of knowing we were going to flip. I couldn't think about the woman who'd just drowned. I couldn't think about the panic of trying to pull her back into the boat, of feeling her hands slip out of mine over and over. I couldn't think about the look in her eyes, or the moment she knew she was going to die in front of her kid. All I could think about was running this rapid, and the rest would come later.

There are these moments on the river when everything crystalizes. It happens in other contexts, too. People call it "flow state." I am a profoundly mediocre athlete, and so I do not regularly experience flow state on skis or when I'm scaling cliffs. But on this particular day, I came as close as I ever have, and probably as close as I ever will.

My paddle was an extension of my very arms; it knew what to do without my thinking about it. It was as if everything in front of me—the roiling whitewater, the sounds of the current and my passengers—narrowed to a tiny pinpoint.

"FORWARD ONE!" I hollered to my crew, and we passed the threshold. We missed the knife by a hair, and, like the proverbial mother lifting a car off a child, I dug in my paddle with more power than I'd realized I had and swung the end of the boat around to river right. One more move, and we'd made it out.

The head boatman nodded almost imperceptibly.

"I think that's the best I've seen anyone run this rapid all season," he granted, and my fellow rookies whooped and congratulated me. I didn't even have time to lean over the edge and throw up; the next rapid was coming up quick.

A few hours earlier, I'd craved that kind of approval. I'd wanted nothing more than to impress the rest of the crew, to be one of the guys. I've kept that compliment close at hand in the years since, pulling it out when I need a reminder that I'm tougher than I think. But there's also something hollow about it—something sad. For me, this was one of those rare before-and-after moments, the ones where our whole perspective flips in a matter of minutes.

So what if I ran it better than anyone else had that season? Could I run it that well again? What about six more times, or a hundred? What about the times it wasn't run perfectly and someone came out of the boat? What if I was the guide who kept trying to pull my client back in, and I couldn't, and they *died*? It was a possibility I couldn't stomach, especially now that I knew it could mean the end of someone's life.

Raft guiding was not shaping up to be the break I'd needed from reality.

Three people died on Clear Creek during the course of my rookie season, and 13 more were killed on other rivers around Colorado that summer.

Statistically, of course, most people who go whitewater rafting aren't killed. Most of them make it to the take-out without incident and tip their guide and go out to lunch and carry on with their day. But thousands of people go rafting every summer with commercial outfits all over the state, some more by the book than others. Even when necessary precautions are taken, an unfortunate reality of recreating in an uncontrollable environment is that a very small percentage of those people are hurt or killed.

To me, it doesn't matter so much how the numbers shake out. The Idaho Springs–based outfit I trained with had an excellent reputation, and for good reason. But after that day at Double Knife, the very real possibility that someone could be killed and I could be directly responsible for that loomed overhead. This was too much for me to bear, which didn't make me a very good candidate to be a raft guide.

So it wasn't exactly *Rocky*. No montages. But two and a half weeks after that day in the Evergreen pool, I'd earned my stripes. I could lift a boat above my head (not effortlessly; they're really heavy) and I'd guided without incident every rapid on that stretch of Clear Creek.

That June, I told the head boatman and the owner I wasn't cut out to guide the creek. They were a little disappointed—I am, after all, terribly charming—but they didn't seem particularly surprised. I guess most people who set out to become raft guides don't stick with it, and then there's all the throwing up I did.

During several of my closest calls on the river, I told myself that if I just survived this one rapid, I'd never set foot on a boat again. This didn't turn out to be true, of course. That sort of bargaining often gives us the strength to make it through a moment, but it's rarely the sort of promise we stick to.

I haven't stayed away from the river. I'd like to say I have a healthy respect for it, but in reality, I am at once terrified of it and drawn to it. For the rest of that summer, I found myself at the shop at least once a week, putting away wetsuits and blowing up boats until someone invited me to paddle with them.

Years later, when my husband and I were getting ready to move from Colorado to Idaho, everyone we knew kept telling us we'd love the rivers.

"You'll have to get a boat," friends kept saying. "That's what people do there in the summer."

"Oh, Emma was a raft guide," Bix would tell them. I never volunteered this information; it felt like lying.

"I guided for a *season*," I'd correct him, though even that didn't feel quite right. I couldn't very well say, "I was scared out of my wits for a season" or "I threw up constantly for three weeks, but really, nothing's wrong with me!"

Still, it wouldn't be quite fair to say I gave up on river tripping after that season. Our honeymoon was down the Green River (that one was Bix's idea), and not long after we made the move to Idaho, we bought a boat.

It's a 14-footer, blue, like the ones I trained on. It's built for comfort, not for speed—just like me. I don't see myself taking it down any Class IV rapids; I think I've mostly gotten that out of my system. Still, I'm very glad I know how to pilot a boat.

Training to be a raft guide was not particularly fun, and I think my close friends and family wondered what the hell was wrong with me. But in doing it, I gave myself a gift. After that summer, I moved through the world with a newfound feeling of confidence. If I could do all that, I reasoned, the next challenge must be, at the very least, survivable.

LESSONS LEARNED

- **Choose a reputable guide.** Like climbing, backcountry skiing, and other high-consequence activities, whitewater sports are best left to those who have some technical training or have a knowledgeable guide. This doesn't completely eliminate the risks; unfortunately, rafters on commercial trips are killed every year. Do plenty of research before choosing an outfitter. Read reviews online—do customers feel safe? Run a quick Google search: Has this outfitter been involved in any high-profile accidents? If so, what do experts say about it—does it appear that they handled the situation appropriately, or is there suspicion that they were negligent? Check to see if they've been sanctioned by the state or local tourism board recreation office, if you have one and those results are public. Watch out for red flags: If you call an outfitter and they seem disorganized or aren't happy to answer your questions, watch out. Do the guides seem happy? Are the boats and vehicles clean and in good condition? Are you asked to sign a waiver, indicating that your outfitter knows the risks and is willing to explain them to you? If the answer to any of these questions is no, they're likely not doing things by the book. Consider taking your trip with someone else.

- **Always wear a life jacket.** Many recreation areas only require that children wear PFDs while on the water, but if you're running whitewater, there's no reason not to. River currents are stronger than any swimmer, and you can use all the extra advantages you can get.

- **Get some training.** Not everyone who runs rivers needs to be a commercially trained raft guide, but if you're headed out all the time—especially on multiday or wilderness trips—someone in your group needs to have some rescue and medical training. Lots of backcountry travelers also choose to get Wilderness First Aid or Wilderness First Responder training. The farther you choose to recreate from potential help, the more important it is that someone has swiftwater rescue training, which could become important should your boat become stranded midriver. At the very least, folks in your group should be CPR certified. It's cheap, doesn't take more than an afternoon, and could absolutely save a friend's (or your) life.

CHAPTER FIVE

Escape from Waimanu Valley

I AM NOT THE SORT OF PERSON WHO CAN EASILY RELAX. IT'S RARE that I'm not worried about something—how things might go wrong, who might be annoyed with me, what work I've left unfinished. Most nights, I lay awake for some time, making a mental checklist of everything I need to accomplish the next day. This is certainly not my favorite thing about myself, and though I've done a great deal of work to try and correct it, I've come to accept that it is embedded in my very genetic makeup and is unlikely to disappear altogether.

As I dug my toes into the black sand beach at the mouth of Waimanu Valley, though, I was very much that sort of person—footloose and fancy-free. How could I not be? I was on Hawaii's Big Island, a slice of paradisiacal rainforest thousands of miles from my unpleasant job and (related) existential dread. After nine miles of strenuous hiking, I was also dead tired.

Unimaginably turquoise waves lapped at my feet as I rummaged around in my backpack for my book—a treatise on surfing my husband had insisted I'd like, though I have no interest in being that far from shore with no life jacket. (Has he not heard of sharks? Riptides? Also, I'm not much of a swimmer.)

"This is my kind of beach vacation," Bix said, sidling up to put his arm around my shoulders. We'd worked hard to get to Waimanu Valley, and it had paid off: There wasn't another person in sight.

As we turned to look at the emerald-carpeted 2,000-foot walls of Waimanu Valley, dotted with shimmering silvery waterfalls, the gathering clouds overhead gave us pause. Bix suggested we put up the tent, and though I'd hoped to sleep out and see the stars, I reluctantly agreed.

Moments later, the skies opened up. I was in for a lesson about the rainforest.

To get to Waimanu Valley, we'd arranged to be dropped off at the Waipi'o Valley Lookout, perched 900 vertical feet above its name-sake black sand beach. My parents drove us there; they have, by now, come to understand that any family vacation involving Bix necessarily includes a day or two off the beaten path. A few weeks earlier, as we'd researched our trip, Bix tried to sell me on Waimanu without explicitly saying that he'd read it was one of the wildest and most remote backpacking destinations on the Big Island. Eventually, despite that I'd initially envisioned a trip revolving primarily around sipping mai tais on the beach, I got into the spirit of things and reserved us a permit for the Muliwai Trail.

Before we even got to the start of the trail, we crossed a calf-deep stream and tromped across picturesque Waipi'o Beach.

"You sure you don't want to just stay here?" I joked, watching a couple of surfers catch head-high waves in the distance.

Bix chuckled, and as I looked over to make a face, I noticed something in the jungle behind him. Gray and clearly human made, it didn't fit in with the towering trees and lush greenery. I stared for a long time, fascinated.

"It's an altar," Bix said quietly, following my gaze.

Waipi'o was the boyhood home of Kamehameha, who would become the first king to rule the entire Hawaiian island chain. It's sometimes called "the Valley of the Kings." There's speculation that it was one of the first outposts established by Polynesian settlers, likely sometime between 300 and 600 AD. These settlers brought the crops, tools, animals, and agricultural techniques they used back home, and some 500 years later, settlements at Waipiʻo and Waimanu likely supported 250 to 500 people.

Waipiʻo would continue to be important in Hawaiian history over the ensuing centuries. In the early 1600s, it was the site of Pakaʻalana, the royal court of King Liloa, and in 1791, the bloody battle of Kepuwahaulaula, between the residents and pillaging invaders, took place at the entrance to Waipiʻo Valley.

One of the most detailed accounts of Waipiʻo Valley's origins is that of missionary William Ellis, who toured Waipiʻo in 1823 with the intention of establishing a missionary station there. He guessed that 1,325 residents lived in 265 houses in the valley. By then, the residents would have had centuries to build stone aqueducts to irrigate their taro fields and fishponds to store food.

Waipiʻo enjoyed thousands of years of bountiful agricultural production, but in 1946, a deadly tsunami wiped out most of the valley. Most of the valley's residents moved away in the wake of the destruction, and it would be another 20 years or so before people started to move back. All told, 50 generations after those Polynesian settlers arrived, Waipiʻo is home to about 50 permanent residents today.

In all those generations, of course, there lived plenty of ancestors for whom to build altars. One such ancestor is Lonoikamakahiki, a seventeenth-century king whose body was kept at the Bishop Museum in Honolulu until 1994, when a group of activists reclaimed his bones and reburied them in Waipiʻo. Given that my guidebook had warned me that Waipiʻo locals are skeptical of outsiders to begin with—understandable, since most have chosen to live there for its relative isolation—I didn't want to intrude by stepping too close to the altars.

I couldn't shake the uneasy feeling I'd gotten from walking past the stone structures, but I was soon distracted by the beginning of the nine-mile Muliwai Trail, which, it turned out, was no joke. The trail cuts a gigantic Z shape with two switchbacks up the valley wall, and when you get to the top of that, the hiking has only just begun.

"This region of Hawaii Island receives over 100 inches of rain annually," the Hawaii Department of Natural Resources' permitting website informs visitors. It also ticks off a handful of other difficulties you might encounter: slippery footing and falling rocks during rain; flash floods; potentially fatal stream crossings; high winds, which may cause branches to fall on the trail or in campsites; and the presence of leptospirosis and hepatitis in untreated water. Oh, and there are feral pigs in the valley.

"Sounds like fun," I'd said to Bix when we first looked at the website. Despite my reticence to encounter any of the hazards listed, I wasn't particularly worried. At this point, we'd both worked as outdoor professionals for the better part of a decade, and our combined experience, thanks to mostly good communication, was greater than the sum of our parts. I was pretty sure we could handle an overnight backpacking trip in beautiful, tropical Hawaii.

After the climb, things eased up for a few minutes. It was humid, but the sky was clear and it wasn't quite so hot in the shade. The trail loosely follows along a single contour line and zigzags into 13 gulches along the way. Most of them are punctuated on either side by a warning sign telling hikers to retreat in case of rain, which is sure to cause flash flooding and also rockfall. An unhappy-looking stick figure who's just been hit in the head with a rock illustrates this point.

With no rain in the forecast for Honoka'a, the nearest town for which I'd been able to find hourly weather updates online, we forged ahead. Nine passionfruit- and lychee-littered miles later, we arrived on the banks of the Waimanu River. It was a relatively comfortable hip high on me, not that I really noticed. I was too distracted by what was on the other side: a black-sand beach framed by palm trees and bookended by the valley's impossibly green walls—and not another soul in sight. I dropped my pack unceremoniously at the perfect campsite and started looking for somewhere to read.

Of course, I didn't get to spend much time enjoying the beach. We'd barely gotten the fly on the tent when the rain started to fall, and it didn't take long for things outside to get very, very wet.

We spent an hour or so playing gin rummy and waiting for the rain to let up. When it didn't, we weighed our options.

Since federal regulations prohibit flying with any kind of fuel, we'd left the stove at home and opted to cook over a campfire. This hadn't looked like a problem, according to the forecast I'd consulted that morning. Now, though, we had a raw onion, a potato, and a local sausage I'd bought in town ("Think this is made of feral pigs?" Bix had asked)—and no way to cook them.

"This'll make a good story," I said, opening a package of Pop-Tarts for dinner. "After all those nights we've spent outside, we're stuck in the rainforest with no stove."

Six rounds of gin rummy later, the game had worn thin, in part, perhaps, because I'm a very sore loser. Bix peeked outside, as if the constant thrum of rain on the fly didn't tell us everything we needed to know about the weather.

By 8:00 p.m., hours after darkness had fallen on the equatorial Big Island, the rain showed no sign of letting up. I took a swig from my almost-empty Nalgene—we'd planned to refill and purify from waterfalls, a no-go in the downpour—and fell asleep to the sound of waves crashing on the beach.

The rain let up sometime before dawn. Bix woke up before me. He said he hadn't gotten much sleep—plagued by guilt for having cheated me at cards, I was sure—and crept out of the tent to take a peek at the river.

"How's it look?" I asked, snooping around in hopes of finding some dry wood to make a fire. When he didn't answer, I looked up, assuming he hadn't heard. His face looked white.

"We should get a move on," he said.

Moments later, I stood on the banks of the swollen Waimanu, which had risen a whopping three feet from yesterday. The previously lazy river had picked up speed, too, but that wasn't the worst of it. Downstream, the river spilled into the ocean, dirtying the perfect azure waves with sediment and mud. I could see exactly how far into the sea I'd end up if I lost my grip mid-crossing.

We unbuckled our pack straps, linked arms, and started across. A third of the way in, the river bottom fell away, and the water reached my chin. To quell the panic rising in my throat, I tightened my grip on Bix's arm and stabbed my trekking pole into the mud, hoping against hope that I wouldn't be swept into the Pacific.

By the time we reached the far shore, I was swimming as hard as I could. When I arrived, I collapsed in the damp sand, shaking uncontrollably despite the humid jungle air. I hoped that was the worst of it, but if my time in the wilderness has taught me anything, it's that luck favors the prepared. I didn't fall into that category in terms of food, water, or a backpacking stove, but there wasn't much I could do about it now. I steeled myself for a tough nine-mile return trip.

The water spraying from each of the 13 gulches was muddier and more forceful than the last. What had been puddles the day before now reached my knees, thighs, hips. Halfway back, an enormous tree had fallen across the trail; newly fallen rocks were scattered across the Muliwai like passionfruit.

The last gully before the descent to Waipi'o Beach featured a 30-foot waterfall where we'd stopped to fill our water bottles the day before. It had been transformed overnight into a firehose, blasting so much muddy water so quickly that we could feel it from 10 feet away. The trail crossed the base of the falls; below that was a slick, mossy 70-foot drop. A fall here would almost certainly be fatal. I swallowed hard—this was it, and then, I figured, we were home free.

My relief at braving the waterfall was short-lived. As we reached the top of yesterday's steep switchbacks, the view of Waipiʻo Beach opened up. A thousand feet below, I could see the little stream we'd crossed before. But it wasn't a stream anymore.

As we'd later find out, the Waipiʻo River drains not only the entire valley, but several others around it; when it rains, those majestic waterfalls empty their contents into the Waipiʻo. Yesterday's clear tidepool, which hadn't even reached my knees, had become a series of opaque standing waves. It was now a Class III rapid I'd be nervous to run in a boat, given the consequences.

We reached the edge of the river, which crumbled away beneath our feet. Without discussion, we dropped our packs and began searching for a way across. Bix started to walk into the current; almost immediately, he lost his balance and thrashed his way to shore. The Waimanu had been bad enough; there was no way we could make it to the other side by linking arms and hoping for the best.

Bix hiked upstream while I scoped out the point where the river met the sea. We reconvened at our packs and shook our heads in unison. For the first time in my life, I began to think I might need a rescue.

We would not have been the first—nor would we be the last— party to find ourselves in this situation. A year and a half after we returned from this trip, an essay I'd written about it appeared on a well-known outdoor podcast, *The Dirtbag Diaries*. Another outdoor educator commented to say she and her partner had had an identical experience on the Muliwai Trail, and another commenter who lived in Hawaii added that this kind of thing happens frequently, since everyone assumes backpacking somewhere this gorgeous will be a walk in the park. (Guilty!)

Unfortunately, not everyone is as lucky as we were. In late August 2019, a 27-year-old man, whose family described him as an experienced hiker, told his father he planned to hike the Muliwai (also called the "Z Trail," thanks to its switchbacks) alone. Somewhere on the trail, he vanished, and as of this writing, no sign of him has been found, despite his family's desperate search.

Weather reports from Waipiʻo in late August and early September 2019 indicated that there was more than zero but less than an inch of precipitation per day during the period when he disappeared, so while it's certainly possible that he encountered trouble crossing a stream, it's impossible to say for sure that that's what happened.

The problem of suddenly rising streams and swift currents isn't unique to the Muliwai Trail or even to the Big Island. The Kalalau Trail, on Kauai's Napali Coast, is regularly closed due to flash flooding. Sometimes, though, the closures don't come soon enough, and hikers are trapped on the wrong side of Hanakapiai Stream. In January 2020, 13 hikers became stranded when the stream flash flooded. Deteriorating weather made it impossible to rescue them by helicopter or boat for days. The Kauai Fire Department was able to deliver some basic supplies early on (the stream crossing is just two miles from the trailhead, so most of the stranded hikers were likely not equipped with overnight gear) and eventually extricated everyone safely.

Everything I knew about flash floods was from a completely different biome. I knew to avoid slot canyons if there was any rain in the forecast, even miles up canyon. These emerald-carpeted walls, I was beginning to understand, funneled excess water in much the same way, despite being much wider and greener than the slot canyons I'd gotten used to back home.

There's one particular flash flood fatality that's always stuck out in my mind. In early August 1963, Roger Clubb Sr. and his eight-year-old son, Roger Jr., set out down the Bright Angel Trail in Grand Canyon National Park. They reached Indian Gardens, four miles below the rim, and rain started to fall heavily—this was monsoon season.

It didn't last long, but when rain falls in the desert, it doesn't just soak into the ground and disappear. In that arid climate, the soil is so unused to excess moisture that it can't absorb inches of rain at a time, and that's where there's soil at all—often it's just sandstone. As the Clubbs were finishing their lunch, a raging river of mud, silt, rocks, and stray branches had begun racing toward them. By the time they heard the earsplitting sound and realized what was happening, it was too late to get out of the way of the 10-foot wall of water.

The elder Clubb rushed to get to high ground but quickly realized his son couldn't keep up. He ran as fast as he could to grab Roger Jr., but his speed was no match for the flood. The roiling wall of sludge engulfed them both, and the Clubbs were never seen alive again. Roger Sr. was found fairly quickly; it would be another five days before his son's body was found.

We sat on our packs. They may be horrifying spectacles if you happen to be in their way, I reasoned, but flash floods pass quickly in the desert. I was still holding out hope that the water would recede after an hour or two and we could cross. We started talking about finding a place to hunker down for the night. I eyed the woods, uneasy about the idea of encroaching on the altars we'd seen the day before, and hoped it wouldn't come to that.

An hour and a half later, the river showed no sign of slowing. I pulled out my book, hoping to use a few pages for kindling, but it, like everything else in my pack—including what remained of our Pop-Tarts—was waterlogged. (Ironically, the inside of my Nalgene was the only dry space in my backpack.)

The panic I'd felt that morning began to spread again. Here I was, a raft guide and backpacking instructor—a professional outdoor educator!—with no food or water, a sopping wet tent and wetter sleeping bag, no way to banish the chills or signal that I needed help. The what-ifs started in. What if we spent another night out and the river didn't subside? What if it rained again?

I stood up and started etching a message in the sand.

"What are you doing?" Bix asked me, perhaps worried I'd really started to lose it this time.

"I'm writing my mom's phone number so someone can call her and tell her we're stuck here," I snapped. Never mind who that someone might be. "If we'd just stayed on a normal beach drinking piña coladas like normal people—"

Then, over the raging torrent, we heard a low whine: a Jeep. This was much more important than the point I'd been trying to make.

We waved our arms and shouted, catching the surfers' attention from the other side of the beach. A muscular Ken doll of a man approached the river and dove in. I was sure I was about to watch him drown, but he appeared on the other side, shook the water from his long, blond hair, and announced that, occasionally, the river came up like this. The surf was excellent today, he informed us.

I picked my jaw up off the beach and introduced myself. We'd been out at Waimanu, I said, and I only dog paddle.

"I can't believe you just swam across that," I told him.

"We're not from around here," Bix explained.

First, the handsome stranger invited us to swim back across. No way, I said. He offered to swim my pack across. I hesitated.

"She wasn't joking about the dog paddling," Bix told him. I averted my eyes, trying not to look sheepish.

Next, he suggested we walk out into the surf and cross in the ocean. There would be a shallow point where the river had built up a sandbar, he explained, allowing us to basically waltz across. He went to demonstrate, making pointed eye contact—*See? No problem*—until the water reached his chin, at which point he must have realized there was no way I could hack it.

I was about to finish etching my mother's phone number into the sand when our would-be hero's buddy appeared in a cheap plastic canoe he'd borrowed from a taro farmer upstream.

"Your chariot, m'lady," he smirked. We deserved that.

We shouldered our packs and loaded up. Laughing riotously as I imitated my swimming technique, our ferry captain deposited us safely on the other side, with the advice that I learn to swim.

The ranger who'd checked our permit the day before was still at his post when we arrived, a little humbler than we'd been the day before, at the Waipi'o Lookout. He said he'd been worried about us with all the rain.

"Me, too," I told him, glad he hadn't had to rescue us. With that, we settled in to play gin rummy until our ride arrived. I finally won a game, and as my prize, Bix agreed that our next trip didn't have to be an epic one.

LESSONS LEARNED

- **Ask a local.** Sometimes, reading the forecast simply doesn't cut it. Without the context provided by local knowledge—namely, that the Waimanu and Waipi'o Rivers drain much of the watershed—we didn't know that despite the lack of rain in the forecast at a nearby town (not located in a valley), we were quite literally in over our waders. I read the permitting website carefully and figured that, along with the forecast and my existing knowledge about backcountry travel, would be plenty to keep me safe. I was wrong, but I was also lucky. Given our rescuers' lack of surprise at the swollen river, it's obvious to me now that this was no isolated incident. I wish I'd called the ranger station to ask about the conditions, searched for local news stories mentioning rescues there, or parsed an online backpacking forum for advice. It's a mistake I won't make in an unfamiliar landscape again.

- **Know where public and private property are.** One of my biggest stressors in this close call was the possibility that we'd have to spend the night on Waipi'o Beach. I'd heard the locals were very private and didn't take kindly to trespassers (rightly so!), and I was really worried about desecrating a monument to someone's ancestor or loved one or trudging upstream on someone's private property to ask for help. I'm grateful it didn't come to that, but now I'm more careful about understanding where private and public land are. Smartphone GPS apps like OnX, typically used for hunting (sportsmen have to be particularly careful about private property in order to hunt ethically and keep their licenses and any game they shoot), are ultraclear about those boundaries; it's worth downloading the maps for the area you'll be traveling in advance. For places that don't have up-to-date GPS information, it's back to the point above—ask a local who knows.

- **Pack enough supplies to wait it out.** I'm not proud of how we handled food on this trip. Between not bringing a stove, assuming we could cook over a fire, and not having enough food for an extra day, this was not my finest moment in planning. I was really hungry by the time we arrived back at the trailhead, but not for one moment was I in danger of starving. Unless you're an ultralight backpacker with the skills and fitness to cover many miles in a day, in which case every ounce counts, there's no reason not to carry one extra freeze-dried meal per person per day. If you're a pretty average backpacker, like me, the extra weight won't make much difference (and if it does, I'd recommend leaving that change of clothes at home). Leaving the camp stove behind, on the other hand, is a gamble—you'd better be pretty damn sure you won't need it. After this incident, it's going to be a long time before mine doesn't make the cut.

- **Be prepared to signal for help.** In this scenario, I was getting ready to etch my mom's phone number into the sand, figuring someone could run up to the lookout, where there's at least spotty service, and give her a call. That was possible only because we were close enough to actually see where we wanted to end up, which of course is not always (in fact, I'd wager, hardly ever) the case when one needs a rescue. Personal locator beacons and satellite phones are spendy, but they're also a much more reliable way to let someone know you're in distress. Each comes with its own set of challenges—PLBs have historically had a nasty habit of going off accidentally, which makes me worry that triggering one might have a boy-who-cried-wolf effect on search and rescue groups. Satellite phones, on the other hand, are very expensive and don't always work in deep canyons or other geographic dead zones. Both technologies are constantly improving, though, and it's worth researching your options before your next remote trip.

- **Have an "Oh shit" time.** Despite my worries, I was comforted throughout my trip back to the trailhead that if we didn't arrive at a specific time, my mom would call in the cavalry. Every time I go into the field, I leave the crucial details of my trip with an in-town coordinator—an institutional habit I've carried into my personal life. It's usually my mom, who is imbued with my same generalized anxiety and whom I can thus count on to call the authorities if need be. I tell her where I'm going, who manages the land I'll be traveling on (the name of the national forest, Bureau of Land Management tract, national park, so forth), the route I intend to follow, and a phone number for the local ranger district. I also calculate an "Oh shit" time: The time by which, if I have not made contact, she should assume things have gone very wrong and I need her to call me a rescue. It's usually sometime the morning after I expect to be out. This gives me time to get to the trailhead on my intended afternoon, drive until I hit cell reception, and give her a call. To date, my mom has never had to call me a rescue. I intend to keep it that way.

Chapter Six

The Wendigo

In northern Minnesota in the dead of winter, a single-digit day is remarkable because it is comparatively balmy. If you were to find yourself in the tranquil North Woods on a day like this, you'd be more likely to encounter temperatures well below zero. Now, on top of that, imagine that you've lost your way in the uniformly dense forest. When you strain to pick up sounds of roads or traffic, you hear only the crystals forming on your exhalations and the crunch of frozen snow beneath your feet.

As you work to collect your thoughts, a stranger appears and offers aid: a warm place to sleep. A mug of hot soup.

This was the story my Midwestern husband told me as we drifted off in the bed of our truck on the too-warm August night before we embarked on my first-ever Boundary Waters trip.

"Tell me about your first trip here," I'd said, assuming he'd come back with a cute story about fishing with his dad. I'd forgotten that my late father-in-law, much like me (and, come to think of it, Bix's mother), had a soft spot for spooky stories and apparently little objection to sharing them with children, regardless of typical standards for age appropriateness.

So Bix launched into a story he'd heard throughout his childhood: A lost or weary traveler in the North Woods who, just as they're about to give in to the elements, is approached by an apparition.

"And then, of course, if you let him help you, you wind up dead," he told me matter-of-factly.

Oh. Of course.

The Wendigo, he explained, stealthily wanders the remote woods in search of human souls to devour. It waits until its victims are at their weakest, their most desperate for help, and makes them an offer they can't rightly refuse.

I assume this logic is similar to that of the vampire, which, as I understand it, cannot enter a person's house until granted the resident's permission. Otherwise, I wondered aloud, couldn't the Wendigo just eat your soul without first politely asking?

This, Bix assured me, was beside the point.

"If ever you see the Wendigo, just ignore it," he advised, yawning.

I've never been able to find another retelling of the Wendigo story quite like the one the Hazard-Firer household heard growing up—wherein the Wendigo's offer to render aid results in the recipient freezing to death or otherwise expiring of seemingly natural causes—but Bix is not the only child of the Upper Midwest to hear some version of the tale.

The Wendigo's origin story varies. It plays heavily in stories from Algonquian-speaking First Nations people, including the Ojibwe, whose ancestral lands are the Boundary Waters region. The Wendigo is a supernatural being, according to Ojibwe stories, but some versions of Wendigo folklore say humans can also become Wendigos if they resort to cannibalism. (These stories have inspired some contemporary references, too, like the Wendigo's appearance in Stephen King's *Pet Sematary*.)

In less literal iterations, the monster is a manifestation of greed-driven environmental destruction. If that's the case, the Boundary Waters are ground zero for a possible Wendigo sighting: Despite

that the Boundary Waters Canoe Area Wilderness (BWCAW)*
is the country's most visited wilderness area, it's continually under
threat. Several mining companies have filed suit demanding mineral
rights to the edge of the designated wilderness area, which would
allow them to engage in sulfide-ore copper mining. This mining
technique has never been legal in Minnesota. When its tailings are
exposed to water and air, they leach heavy metals and other contam-
inants. It's toxic enough that modeling shows a single mine would
pollute parts of the wilderness area for at least 500 years.

A single mine using this technique, let alone a string of mines,
would invariably change the character of the Boundary Waters, and
not just from a recreational perspective. Aquatic ecosystems, and
in turn the surrounding forests, would suffer or be destroyed altogether. Already-endangered species would be further threatened.
The watershed that encompasses a huge portion of the Upper Midwest would be contaminated with mercury, and local economies
that rely on tourism (a nearly billion-dollar industry with more
than 17,000 jobs in Minnesota alone) would tank. Given all that,
the Wendigo sounds relatively harmless.

It would make a better story to tell you the Wendigo weighed on
my mind as we set off into some of the most remote wilderness in
North America, but if I'm being honest, I had much more pressing

---

* This 150-mile-long stretch on the US–Canada border was designated capital-W Wilderness by
the Boundary Waters Canoe Area Wilderness Act in 1978. The entire area lies within Superior
National Forest, and it's administered by the US Forest Service. It's often abbreviated to the BWCA
or BWCAW, and along with several other areas, including the Superior National Forest, Voyageurs
National Park, and the Quetico and La Verendrye Provincial Parks in Ontario, it makes up the area
I'm referring to throughout this chapter as the Boundary Waters. I'm choosing to call it that rather
than the BWCAW because it's so much more than just a designated wilderness area. It's ecosystems,
natural and human history, and experiences. Referring to it by its wilderness designation risks polit-
icizing something that simply isn't political: The Boundary Waters region is an intrinsically valuable
slice of North America, and we cannot risk losing it.

concerns—what this whole "portage" thing was going to be about, for example, and how our dog Bodhi would do for hours each day in a canoe.

I was right to be more concerned with the tangible. Less than 10 minutes after we put the canoe in the water at Sea Gull Lake, I swore I could hear the telltale sound of a rapid. We rounded a bend in the shoreline, and there it was: a rapid. The kind that belongs in a river.

"We must have read the map wrong," I said, incredulous. I even glossed right over the fact that I was told we would be paddling through a bunch of *lakes*, which are not supposed to have rapids. "This rapid is flowing toward us."

"Nope, this is right," Bix said from the back of the boat.

"Look," I gestured at the rapid. He clearly hadn't understood. "We'd have to paddle it *upstream!*"

This did not appear to faze Bix, who calmly stepped out of the boat and into the knee-deep water, causing the dog to wheel around and look at me, panic-stricken. I shrugged back at him: *I'm as confused as you, bud.*

Bix lined our canoe up the tiny rapid as I clutched the sides of the boat, which I'd been assured was remarkably stable but was now certain would dump its contents, myself and my nervous dog included, into the frigid lake.

This was very different from any boating I'd ever done. Which makes sense, because the Boundary Waters Canoe Area Wilderness is very different from any other place I've ever been. It covers more than a million acres of almost unthinkably remote wilderness, and that's just on the American side. The neighboring Quetico Provincial Park encompasses more than 1,800 additional square miles of intricately linked lakes and rivers.

Bix had been describing this landscape to me since I met him. It sounded nice, but I'd grown up in the Rockies—to me, "rugged wilderness" meant craggy peaks and elevations that require acclimating.

It's not that I doubted the Boundary Waters would be beautiful. I just couldn't picture a different kind of wildness. Within the first hour of my first day on the water, I was starting to get the picture.

It turns out the 17-foot Wenonah canoe we'd borrowed for this trip was, in fact, very stable. As we emerged at the top of the little rapid, I felt a surge of gratitude for this 60-pound hunk of fiberglass and wood. How could I have doubted the noble canoe, iterations of which have been used by cultures across the world for 10,000 years?

My feelings of elation lasted approximately 15 minutes, until we arrived at our first portage. The name "Boundary Waters"—emphasis on the plural *waters*—is an apt description for this area, which comprises some 1,175 lakes of varying sizes. Any route through the Boundary Waters that goes beyond the first-ring lakes, those closest to the designated entry points, requires canoeists to unload their boats, stuff all their gear into a portage pack, and carry said gear and the boat across a stretch of land to the next lake.

This process is exactly as tedious as it sounds, and the only member of our party who actively looked forward to it was Bodhi, who was not required to lug any of his own gear and was thus thrilled with any excuse to stretch his legs. If you do not happen to be a carefree dog, even the lightest canoe feels awfully heavy when you're carrying it over your head, and a portage pack full of all the gear two people need for a week in the wilderness can tip the scales at 100 pounds, easy.

Portages are measured in "rods," or units of 16.5 feet—the length of your average canoe. A portage of a few dozen rods is one thing; a portage of a few hundred rods requires a bit more fortitude. (The longest single portage on this route was a respectable 209 rods.)

But it's not just the length you have to consider. Some portages are on relatively flat, well-maintained trails, while others are unmarked or rocky or steep or even, as I'd soon discover, through a swamp filled with oozing, thigh-deep mud.

Fortunately, our first portage of the day was the former. I'm not sure what I was picturing, exactly, but there was something demoralizing about unpacking the boat we'd so carefully rigged just half an hour earlier.

"You want the canoe or the pack?" Bix asked.

Carrying the canoe sounded more glamorous, so I picked that. It did not take me long to discover, however, that hoisting the canoe overhead and carrying it for any distance were two very different things. To say I carried the canoe a full rod from where we pulled it from the water before sheepishly asking to trade would be very generous.

The heavy portage pack was more my speed. My backpacking and mountaineering experience meant I knew how to put my head down and keep putting one foot in front of the other. Soon enough, much to Bodhi's disappointment, it was time to reload the boat and paddle toward our next portage.

Are we really going to have to do this every time? I wondered. (We really were.)

As much as I grew to dread portaging on this trip—and I did—I was grateful each time we found the path we were looking for. Some Boundary Waters portages are super obvious, particularly on the relatively well-traveled lakes we paddled on this particular loop. On the most frontcountry lakes, you might pick out a portage by the sight of another party loading their boats. Farther in, the presence of a trail is generally a good indication that following it will get you somewhere.

A couple of times, though, we had to look hard to find a portage. I'd think I was looking at a trail, and after a few yards, it would peter out—a game trail, useful for deer but not humans looking to transport a canoe to another lake.

In August 1998, Dan Stephens, a 22-year-old guiding a group of Boy Scouts and a couple of their leaders, was looking for a flat, 21-rod portage. The path would take his group into Bell Lake, just north of Saganaga Lake loop, on the Canadian side of the border in Quetico Provincial Park. The portage was notoriously difficult to find, unmarked on Stephens's map—and it didn't help that this was his first time paddling this particular chain of lakes. Stephens had some beta from another guide, and he was adept at orienteering, so he got his group settled and headed off to find the portage.

Hours later, when he hadn't returned, the group started to worry. They were right to be concerned: Stephens had gotten turned around, then fallen off a granite boulder and passed out. Upon waking he wandered through the woods for three days using his knowledge of the area (he knew the general direction he needed to go) and a rudimentary navigational technique before eventually encountering a separate group of Scouts and being rescued.

Stephens got lucky, and it helped that he had a fair amount of outdoor experience. Maps have come a long way since 1998, not to mention the advent of GPS technology. You should have both with you in the Boundary Waters, and you shouldn't leave the vicinity of your canoe without, at the very least, a compass—the best way to survive getting lost here is to not get lost in the first place.

By the time we made it to a little inlet of Saganaga Lake to look for a campsite, I was thoroughly convinced of the ruggedness of the Boundary Waters. Already I was beginning to see that while Labor Day Weekend might pass for fall elsewhere, it was still really just late summer here. I'd been assured the bugs would be far fewer in number by now, but they were still biting. I'd like to say I appreciated the wild beauty of the landscape, but really, I was ready to eat dinner and collapse into my mosquito-free tent.

That's not to say my first night in the Boundary Waters was entirely unpleasant. Unlike where I grew up, where most summers are so dry that a single cigarette butt or spark from a braking freight train can set thousands of acres on fire, campfires are a staple of Midwestern camping. (Forest fires are certainly possible in the Boundary Waters—if you've read this far, you know I've considered the gamut of potentially fatal hazards, and I'll get to that one shortly.)

Bix built a smoky fire to shoo the mosquitoes away, and after two-thirds of a bag of Sour Patch Kids, I made short work of setting up the tent. I was too tired to chop veggies or sauté anything (I'd offered to cook dinner, usually a Bix job, so he could spend the afternoon fishing), so we watched the sun set over heaping bowls of tuna mac. Our post-dinner cleanup was serenaded by loon calls, which I had never heard before and which are so eerie and sad and beautiful I was almost moved to tears, although that could have been aided by my portage-sore shoulders.

We managed to stay up long enough to see the stars, including my favorite constellation, Cassiopeia, who makes her appearance in the northern sky each fall. Because the Midwest believes deeply in hospitality and was determined to show me a good time, I fell asleep to the sound of wolves howling in the distance. Even Bodhi was too tired to care.

Sometime in the wee hours, I thought I heard thunder. In the Rockies, thunderstorms roll in like clockwork most afternoons, so the sound itself didn't worry me. But when I heard it a second time, it was loud enough to rouse me from my comatose sleep. I nudged Bix, who was snoring soundly next to me.

"There's thunder!" I hissed. He mumbled something and rolled over.

Lightning flashed, and my Colorado-kid habit of counting until the thunder rolled, five seconds for every mile away the storm was, kicked in. *One, t—*

"*Wow*, it's right on top of us, huh?" Bix said, rolling over to face me.

"Should we check on the boat?" I asked, certain the water would come up, sweep our canoe into Saganaga Lake, and leave us stranded.

"Nah," Bix yawned. "It's just an electrical storm. This happens all the time."

For those keeping score at home, so far on this romantic Boundary Waters trip Bix has planned, there are: Hordes of mosquitoes and black flies, crotch-high quicksand, nightly electrical storms directly on top of us (!), and, debatably, a homicidal demon who, according to various oral histories, may or may not require permission to devour my soul. Got it. Bix has only bothered to warn me about the last thing, and honestly, the Wendigo is the least of my worries right now.

A little higher on my list of worries is that, in these strong winds, a tree will topple onto our tent. Finding a spot to put the tent is usually my job (it beats cooking), and I take it very seriously. I'm not crazy about this wind, but when I run through my mental checklist, I know I've picked a relatively safe spot for us to sleep.

When I pick a site, I start up close, then zoom out. First of all, I'm thinking about Leave No Trace guidelines. I'm looking for a spot at least 200 feet from water and ideally just as far from my kitchen area. I want a durable surface—no cheery wildflowers to smash or anthills to decimate. I also want it to be flat and level and not in a spot that will collect water if it rains.

You don't want to be within reach of a tree that's likely to fall, so finding the perfect tent site also requires you to think like an arborist. Dead and leaning trees are a no-go; on nearby live trees, I'm keeping an eye out for branches that look like they might break.

In the summer of 2016, a man was killed near Duncan Lake when he, his son, and a third man sought shelter from one of these big, powerful storms. A large tree—a mature white pine—was knocked over by the strong winds. The tragic incident was especially high profile because the victim, Craig Walz, was the brother of a US congressman. His teenage son was also seriously injured, though he survived. That storm was a doozy; the same night, another man was struck and injured by a falling tree on Clove Lake, near the Canadian border.

You can certainly minimize your odds of being injured or killed by blowdown by avoiding dead trees. But, unfortunately, in a storm like that, being hit by a falling tree is a matter of being in the wrong place at the wrong time.

Twenty minutes later, the rain had not let up, and I would classify its intensity as "torrential." When the first droplet of water hit me square between the eyes, I sighed loudly in an attempt to wake up my husband, whom I hoped would venture into the maelstrom and restake the tent fly. When he didn't respond, I rolled over abruptly, elbowing him in the side. He started.

"Oh, good, you're awake!" I feigned surprise. "Anyway, it's dripping."

At this point, Bix had been married to me long enough to assess the situation while only half awake. To his credit, he appeared to harbor no ill will as he rummaged for his shoes and unzipped the tent door, letting half a dozen biting insects in.

"Don't you want pants?" I asked helpfully, slapping at a mosquito as I slunk back into my sleeping bag.

"They'll just get wet," he shrugged, and with that, he staggered outside in his underpants to batten down the hatches.

I've spent enough time above tree line with Bix that I wasn't particularly worried about him being struck by lightning—he knows how to tell when it's close, and he knows what to do if it is—but it does happen in the Boundary Waters.

In summer 2016—in fact, during the same storm as the incidents involving falling trees—a group of Outward Bound students camped on Crooked Lake in Sunday Bay, just north of Ely. The group's two leaders had done everything right and spread the group out, but lightning struck a nearby stand of trees (virtually unavoidable on land in the Boundary Waters, especially since you don't want to be the tallest thing around) and injured three group members. Injuries ranged from superficial burns to loss of consciousness, but no one was killed and the party was rescued and taken to Ely to recover.

Just over three years later, a party of nine Girl Scouts was rescued from Knife Lake, five portages from their starting point, after experiencing ground current when lightning struck nearby. No one was struck directly or injured, but the three adults and six teens were likely terrified by the near miss.

We know about these two near misses because organizational protocols often require group leaders to report lightning strikes, and when an injury happens in an institutional setting, there are systems in place to rescue those folks. Given the frequency of electrical storms in this area, the likelihood that you'll see lightning during the summer in the Boundary Waters is good, though if you follow lightning best practices, you can probably avoid necessitating a rescue. (I say "probably" because there's a degree of uncertainty with lightning. At this point, dear reader, you surely know there's no way to *guarantee* safety in the backcountry.)

The first and most important thing to know about lightning in the Boundary Waters is that if you see it, you should get off the water. There's a reason suburban outdoor pools close for lightning: Water is a conductor, and you do not want to be in the middle of it if it's struck by a current carrying a billion volts of electricity.

Once you're on land, you want to avoid being the tallest object in the vicinity. Find a stand of trees to hide under. Avoid caves or rock overhangs, which are tempting for their solidity but can carry ground currents when lightning strikes nearby. Spread out from the rest of your group, as electrical currents can strike and travel between multiple human bodies. Crouch down in a "lightning position," on the balls of your feet, with your feet touching. This reduces the risk of a current traveling through one foot, up your leg, through your body, and out through the other foot. Wrap your arms around your knees—you want as little of your body touching the ground as possible, as it's an excellent conductor, especially when wet. If you have a sleeping pad available, crouch on that. This will be uncomfortable, especially if you need to hold the position for a long time. But it's definitely better than being struck by lightning.

The prospect of being struck by lightning is objectively terrifying, but it's not exactly likely. The National Weather Service estimates that your odds of being struck at some point during your lifetime are 1 in 15,300, and just 10 percent of those struck by lightning are killed by it.

A more common scenario, unfortunately, has consequences on a much larger scale: the dreaded forest fire. Throughout the Boundary Waters region, forest fires have long been a part of the ecosystem's natural lifecycle, but modern fire suppression efforts have changed the phenomenon's frequency and seriousness. The 1999 Boundary Waters blowdown, caused by a storm whose winds reached up to 100 miles per hour, resulted in millions of downed trees over 350,000 acres—perfect for starting gigantic wildfires.

In addition to finding that fuel loads on the forest floor had increased dramatically, the Forest Service determined that, in general,

> lightning strikes will be more successful at igniting wildfires in the blowdown, and that fires are more likely to exhibit extreme behavior. . . . Fires will be larger and will spread more quickly under more moderate weather conditions because of the high fuel density, the potential for plume-dominated fire, and the difficulty in controlling wildfires in the blowdown.

Several fires have taken place in the Boundary Waters since the 1999 blowdown. The most notable to date was the Pagami Creek Fire, which was caused by a lightning strike in August 2011. It smoldered for a few days in a bog, producing very little smoke, a common phenomenon with lightning-caused fires. Then winds picked up and humidity dropped, and the fire blew up. By mid-September, it encompassed more than 92,000 acres. Its 35,000-foot-high plume created its own weather system; smoke drifted as far south as Chicago. It was the largest wildfire in Minnesota in more than a century.

At least one couple had a near miss with the Pagami Creek Fire. It had moved slowly at first, and though rangers had closed a swath of the Boundary Waters and were monitoring the situation, much of the region appeared to be safe. These 20-year Boundary Waters veterans had checked in with rangers, then embarked on a 10-day trip. Two days in, when they were on Kawasachong Lake, the wind picked up and smoke had started to linger, and a quick reconnaissance showed that the fire was right on top of them. They survived by abandoning their camp and paddling into the middle of the lake; when one of them was thrown from their boat, the other jumped in, and they both ended up treading water. Finally, when they were nearly hypothermic, the fire around them was dampened by a torrential downpour. They survived an uncomfortable night with just the gear they'd hurriedly grabbed from their campsite and paddled out the next morning.

If you learn only one thing from this book, I hope it's this: You should always know the risks associated with the specific route you're planning to take. Nowhere does this hold more true than in the Boundary Waters, thanks to the region's vastness and remoteness. You definitely will not have cell service to stay up to date on the status of any fires that happen to be in the area.

First, familiarize yourself with the region impacted by the 1999 blowdown. If you'll be traveling within it—if you're in the central and eastern portions of the BWCAW—there's an increased risk of wildfire, so you'll need to be hypervigilant about doing your part to prevent forest fires. This is pretty straightforward: Don't start a campfire (or put an already-lit one out) if it's windy, and always keep campfires to a manageable size. Never leave a campfire unattended, and make sure fires are dead out when you turn in for the night. (This holds true even if it looks like it's going to rain—is it really worth the risk?)

You also need to be prepared to react if you do encounter a fire. If you see or smell smoke, reevaluate your trip plan. Keep a close eye on the weather, particularly on the wind—prevailing winds mean most fires in this region head north and east, but it's possible that changes in wind direction will blow a fire in other directions. Check the map and plan an alternative route to give the smoke you're seeing a wide berth, preferably one that takes you through a large body of water. The best times of day to travel may be early in the morning and late at night, when conditions tend to be most humid.

Stick close to the biggest lakes possible in case you find yourself in the midst of a wildfire. In this case, make sure your personal flotation device (PFD) is secure and paddle to the middle of the lake. Here's the part where you'll have to fight against your natural instincts: Get out of the boat and into the water. Tip over your canoe and stay underneath it, where cooler, less smoky air will be trapped. (Your life jacket is key here—save your energy by having it keep you afloat rather than treading water.)

If you're in this situation, you'll almost certainly need to travel across a freshly burned area to get out of the wilderness. Be vigilant: There may still be burning embers on the ground, and stump holes can still be hot enough to burn you. The trees around you may be very fragile, so steer clear to the best of your ability; with their roots burned, they're far less stable and liable to fall. If you have just survived a wildfire in the Boundary Waters, I don't need to tell you this, but *move quickly.*

The morning after the storm, most of our gear was very, very wet. This was mostly fine; our food was kept dry in a bear-proof barrel, and after Bix's heroic efforts, the contents of our tent were relatively dry. Within a few hours, everything would air out in the heat of the day or be soaked in sweat, so it wasn't really a problem. Still, I resolved to run a tighter ship at the next night's camp.

Over the next couple of days, we settled into a rhythm. Days started and ended with the activities familiar to me: make coffee, break camp; set up a tent, cook dinner, read, or, in Bix's case, fish. (He didn't catch a thing all week. He assures me that fish in the Boundary Waters are notoriously fickle, and as a personal favor to him I have never made any effort to fact-check this assertion.) The meat of the day, on the other hand, took some getting used to: rig boat, paddle, unload boat, portage, repeat.

Soon, even Bodhi had resigned himself to his status as a boat dog. On Sea Gull Lake, in perhaps the proudest moment of Bix's adult life, we paddled past an old-timer in a solo canoe, who waved, whistled, and shouted, "Now, there's a dog who knows how to ride a canoe!" Imagine this in the most up-north Midwestern accent you can muster.

We had a couple more electrical storms at night, but each morning dawned sunny and clear, and there was virtually no wind as we paddled from one campsite to the next. Bix had told me that the waves on the bigger lakes could "kick up pretty good." But considering that none of the dangers he'd actually warned me about had been much of anything—no Wendigo sightings, probably at least in part because I refused to leave the safety of the tent at night—I hadn't lent this possibility much credence.

So when I woke up to overcast skies on the last morning of our trip, I was incredulous. I took my time getting dressed and tearing down the tent.

"What's up with this weather?" I asked Bix, who had been up fishing for an hour and was currently heating water for the French press. "It'll burn off, right?"

"'Burn off?' This isn't Colorado, babe," he chuckled. "This is the Midwest. It'll be like this till spring now."

This was obviously an exaggeration, which Bix is quite prone to. But as is usually the case with his overstatements, there was a kernel of truth to it: Midwestern skies spend much of the fall and winter in a state I would call *oppressively gray*. And while it's often gloomy but not threatening, on this particular morning, the wind was already ripping ominously through the branches over our campsite. At least this meant no mosquitoes.

As much as I wasn't in a hurry to leave the relative comfort of camp, I didn't relish the thought of being on the lake any later in the day than I had to—I was ready to get this thing over with. I cinched my PFD extra tight, then did the same to Bodhi's.

"This will be fine," I told him as he wriggled away from me, suddenly interested in some scent just out of reach. This reassurance was for me, really. The dog wasn't worried. He knew how to ride a canoe.

Once we were out on the water, it didn't take long for me to understand that Bix had not been exaggerating about the lakes' ability to kick up waves. Twenty minutes into our paddle, white-caps had begun to form, and it took all our combined concentration to keep the canoe perpendicular to the growing waves.

There are no formal, published records on annual accidents or drownings in the BWCAW, but consider that a summer rarely passes without news of at least one drowning in the Boundary Waters. They happen in lakes big and small, in high winds and on calm days, when people are traveling solo or with a group of friends. The common thread? Very frequently, when people drown in the Boundary Waters, they are not wearing a life jacket.

Look, I get it. They can be uncomfortable, especially on a hot, sticky summer day. They don't look especially cool. And if you're a strong swimmer or grew up without using one, it can be hard to get into the habit.

But here's the thing: No matter how strong a swimmer you are, you are better equipped to keep your head above water if you're wearing a PFD. Period. Even in summer, the water temperature is chilly, usually topping out in the 60s Fahrenheit (your average swimming pool is in the 80s). That's at the height of summer. In June, you might find the water on the bigger lakes is in the 40s. Even an Olympic swimmer would have a physiological reaction to suddenly being plunged into water that temperature, and you can't swim very well when you're hypothermic. Put simply: If you're on the water, wear a life jacket.

Our last campsite had been on an island, so we paddled hard to get close to the nearest shoreline. Sticking closer to the water's edge would add a little mileage to the day, but this seemed a worthwhile tradeoff. I am willing to go to great lengths to reduce the amount of swimming I'll theoretically have to do.

Fortunately, it didn't come to that. The whitecaps certainly got my adrenaline pumping, but after 30 minutes of hard paddling, we'd reached a narrow channel into a more protected cluster of islands, and the waves dissipated.

As we neared our starting point at Trails End Campground, Sea Gull Lake began to look different. Motorized craft are allowed on parts of the lake, and despite the dreary weather, we passed half a dozen boats on our approach to the ramp. I guess an overcast day can't be much of a deterrent from getting outside during a Midwestern autumn, or you'd spend most of the season indoors.

Trails End is literally the end of the Gunflint Trail, and it sees a fair amount of traffic during the peak season. When we pulled up to the boat ramp, Bodhi leapt from the boat as if it was on fire, making a beeline for a rotting fish carcass floating lazily in the shallows. Two little girls from the family unloading in front of us squealed, delighted at the sight of a dog in a life jacket.

Despite being chilly, damp, and very hungry, I couldn't help but smile. The Boundary Waters are a vast, rugged wilderness accessible not just to hardy adventurers, but to families with little kids and groups of friends on annual fishing trips, like the guys putting in as we pulled our boat from the water. It's also steeped in natural and human history—a few hours in the Boundary Waters is plenty long enough to understand why paddling here is often likened to taking a journey through time.

On a dark, ferociously rainy night, it's not hard to see where the story of the Wendigo came from. The truth is, the Wendigo is not an external force: We each have a limit, a moment at which we don't believe we can possibly endure the heat or cold or hunger or exhaustion any longer. We can push those internal limits, augment them with practice and proper gear, and know when they're approaching so we can start making our way home. The best way to keep the Wendigo at bay isn't to avoid the North Woods. It's to go into them prepared—and protect them for all we're worth.

LESSONS LEARNED

- **Start small.** When Bix and I first started planning this trip, he suggested a 25-mile loop to be covered in five days. This was a distance we'd easily covered on an overnight backpacking trip. "You don't have to baby me," I told him. But there's more to a Boundary Waters trip than meets the eye. Portaging adds time and saps energy. Paddling even a few miles can take hours in a headwind. Navigating can be tricky and require backtracking. If you're new to this area, a short, manageable loop is ideal. You've never been anywhere quite like this before.

- **Get good—really good—at navigating.** By the time I embarked on my first Boundary Waters trip, I'd navigated my way through hundreds of miles of terrain ranging from trackless desert to vast glacial wilderness. I was really good at reading a map. But this place challenged me in a way I didn't expect. It always takes a little time (and trial and error) to calibrate your brain to the scale of a place. This is no exception, and you move at a different pace on the water than you do on foot. The way an island or shoreline looks from the seat of a canoe might be quite different from how it appears from a bird's-eye view on the map. I always recommend bringing a paper map and compass *and* a reliable GPS device. If that feels like overkill elsewhere, I can't emphasize enough how much it doesn't feel that way here—you really do need them both. Practice orienteering skills before you take off, and be vigilant about monitoring the map and the GPS once you're out on the water.

- **When in doubt, stay put.** Ideally, you'll be a navigational pro by the time you take on a Boundary Waters trip (and remain alert throughout). If you do find yourself lost, though, whether you're in the woods alone or have pulled your canoe ashore because you're not totally sure where you are or where you're headed, don't attempt to find your way out. You *could* get lucky, sure, but you're likelier to worsen the situation. Instead, stay right where you are. If you've filed a trip plan with your permit, or even left a detailed itinerary with a friend or relative, a search party will be able to find you pretty quickly—provided you're still on the route where you said you'd be.

- **Choose your tent site wisely.** Storms in the Upper Midwest are big and powerful. In the Boundary Waters, choosing a campsite is made a little easier by the fact that your permit requires you to camp only at designated sites. This means you don't need to worry about finding a spot a specific number of feet off the water; the Forest Service has done the measuring for you. Sites have a cast-iron fire grate (make your campfires only in these) and a latrine, which is typically easy to find via an established footpath (yep, you guessed it—use the bathroom only in the designated latrine). Within your campsite, though, you'll have to choose a specific spot to pitch your tent. Don't be lulled into complacency by the fact that someone else has camped here before. Look around: Are there dead or leaning trees nearby? Big storms can topple even healthy trees, but you can decrease your chances of being injured or killed by avoiding the trees that will be weakest in a storm.

- **Watch the weather.** Your entry permit entitles you to spend up to 365 days in the BWCAW. That is to say: If the weather's bad or there's a storm building, there's no legal reason you can't stick around for another day until things settle down. You may have a shift scheduled at work or an overdue rental item, but a missed shift or a late fee on your rented Honda pale in comparison to the possibility of a lost life, which could be the consequence of attempting to paddle through the Big One. If you choose to paddle when the weather is unfavorable, show up with a game plan. Look at the map: Where will you pull off along the way if things get too bad to continue? What's the farthest you might have to swim if things go south, and are you capable of doing that? Is your boat rigged to prevent you from losing anything if it flips? Have you packed in such a way that you can easily access what you might need to prevent hypothermia? The more prepared you are, the less likely it is that you'll need it.

Chapter Seven

After the Slide

When you are buried in an avalanche, you literally cannot move an inch.

It's not like the old-timey stories you hear about being "buried alive." No one relishes the idea of waking up in a coffin—walls inches from your face, not enough room to sit up or turn around. This is worse. It's like being buried in a Tempur-Pedic coffin: The snow conforms to your every curve and crevice. And then it sets up like concrete, and you can't readjust your position, let alone dig your way out. It is truly the stuff of nightmares.

Fortunately, if you want to put it that way, you don't have to put up with the nightmare for very long. Contrary to what you might think, most people buried in avalanches don't freeze to death. That process can take hours, maybe longer. Instead, after about 15 minutes, you're much more likely to asphyxiate—you run out of oxygen in your tiny, you-shaped coffin, and that's that.

This is the dark side of recreating in the backcountry in winter. It's what I think about every time I go for a ski tour and why, consequently, I am probably not all that much fun to ski with.

The last chunk of snow falls into place, and suddenly it's dark in my little cave. My breath catches. I am acutely aware of just how alone I am under the snow.

"All good down there?" I hear a muffled voice. It sounds miles away.

"Yep!" I holler back at the top of my lungs.

My radio spurts and sputters and crackles to life. Of course—snow is a great insulator. They can't hear me, no matter how loudly I yell.

"All good in there?" someone's asking me, this time on the radio.

"All set!" I chirp, doing my best not to sound like the sort of person who might panic at the thought of being buried in a snow cave, which as far as I know is everyone.

I'm bundled in a puffy down jacket, stuffed in a sleeping bag, and lying on an insulated pad, so I'm much warmer than, say, someone who moments before had been zipping along on their skis might be. It would actually be pretty cozy, if only my lizard brain would quiet down.

Now it's time for the hard part. The only way to get out of here is to wait.

I did not move to Alaska for graduate school with the intention of studying snow science. I realized immediately after finishing my bachelor's degree that I wasn't going to use my teaching license, and an advanced degree appealed more than my job waiting tables. Alaska sounded exotic, exciting. Ironically, studying snow and the ways people behave in it didn't even occur to me until I was evacuated from a winter wilderness skills course with frostbite.

But it wasn't just the snow itself that got me hooked. Like most people who work in the world of snow and avalanches, I found myself studying what happens in the winter because of a mentor: my graduate advisor, Eeva Latosuo.

Eeva has more energy than most people. If my calculations are correct, she cannot possibly sleep for more than four, maybe five, hours a night. The prolonged darkness of the Alaskan winter doesn't bother her; she is from Finland. Whether it's the result of a life spent at northern latitudes or she's just preternaturally motivated, Eeva manages to get more done in a week than most people do all winter.

Having Eeva as a role model opened doors for me. My second year in Alaska, she introduced me to the new executive director of the Alaska Avalanche School, where I landed an internship and became fully immersed in the winter world.

It was a lot to juggle an internship and a part-time job on top of grad school, but if anyone could make it seem like I had plenty of free time, it's Eeva. In addition to teaching a full class load in Alaska Pacific University's Outdoor Studies department, advising a grad student or two, and instructing multiday courses at the Alaska Avalanche School each winter, Eeva is a dedicated search and rescue (SAR) volunteer. She and her border collie, Sisu (who, as of this writing, holds the altitude record in Alaska for rescue dogs: 11,000 feet), are called out on a handful of searches each season.

This is how I came to be buried in a snow cave at Hatcher Pass, one of south-central Alaska's most popular backcountry skiing and snowmachining* areas.

Every other year, SAR teams from all over Alaska—including the Alaska Mountain Rescue Group, Alaska Search and Rescue Dogs, Alyeska Avalanche Dogs, Anchorage Nordic Ski Patrol, and Mat-Su SAR group—collaborate with local land managers and avalanche forecast centers to run an interagency drill. It is much more complex and involves far more subjects than your average rescue scenario, which is the point: This helps rescue personnel ensure that they're ready for just about anything. Unfortunately, by the time a SAR team steps on the scene of an avalanche accident in real life, it is much more frequently to recover a body than

---

* In the Lower 48, most people refer to these machines as "snowmobiles." They do things differently in Alaska, where everyone calls them "snowmachines."

to rescue a live person. Still, it's important that things can run smoothly during an actual crisis, so the drill is a big deal.

Drills like this serve an important purpose for the dogs, too. Dogs like Sisu are incredibly emotionally intelligent. When they find a deceased subject ("subject" is SAR speak for victim or patient), they are visibly subdued. Perhaps not all dogs are capable of sadness, but as I understand it, Sisu and her canine counterparts are.

Luckily, the inverse is true, as well. Search dogs are ecstatic when they find a live subject, which is why regular practice is a crucial element of their training. It's important that the dogs find a live subject every once in a while—after all, they don't know whether it's a test or the real deal—so they don't burn out. Sometimes their reward is a treat; other times the practice subject goes off into the woods or is buried with a favorite toy. When the subject is found, a fierce game of tug-of-war ensues.

I can tell you about every avalanche fatality that happened between the years 1986 and 2006. It's not exactly a winsome party trick, but there it is.

It didn't come easily. It took editing two volumes of *The Snowy Torrents*, a collection of avalanche accident narratives and analysis published somewhat irregularly by the American Avalanche Association. Now, I've spent hundreds of hours reading—not skimming, but reading in exacting, sometimes excruciating, detail—about the worst days of people's lives.

I've read about a lot of accidents, but not nearly as many as Spencer Logan, Lead Avalanche Scientist at the Colorado Avalanche Information Center (CAIC). In addition to issuing public avalanche forecasts, the CAIC keeps an avalanche accident database for the entire United States, which Spencer has maintained since 2007. I first met him when we worked together on the *Snowy Torrents* volume that catalogs accidents between 1996 and 2004, which he coauthored. As I worked on the book you're reading now, I asked him what patterns he'd picked out in all those years of investigating and writing about accidents. I figured if anyone could tell me a magic spell for avoiding an avalanche accident, it was Spencer.

"It's a big question, because there are patterns we can see in hindsight—where we can see the information people missed or the mistakes they made," he explained. "Those hindsight patterns are easy to pick out: underestimating the avalanche potential, overestimating the ability to escape, not being aware of where you are."

But humans, Spencer points out, are great at justifying our decisions, and so the patterns are tougher to pick out from the points of view of those involved. Victims may not feel like they are missing information, he says. That's where we start seeing the human factors, like being overly committed to a goal or feeling social pressure to take risks you otherwise might not.

"That's why having several perspectives is important," he told me. "When we're looking back on accidents with a lot of information or our own preconceptions, we can see patterns. When we're looking at what people were *experiencing* and trying to understand that, we can see somewhat different patterns." Combining those perspectives can add to our understanding of how and why things went wrong.

So, no magic spell. Avoiding an accident takes significant, ongoing effort.

Most of the time, that Worst Day begins ordinarily. People wake up early, excited to go skiing. Sometimes it's been a slow snow year, and this is slated to be a sunny day after the first big storm in a while. What could be better than that?

But things can fall apart before you even leave the house.

Sometimes it's the conditions. There's no way to know for sure how many avalanches occur in the United States every year; most go unwitnessed and unreported (if a tree falls in the forest and there's no one around to hear it, and all that). Avalanches need three ingredients in order to take place: a bed surface, a cohesive slab of snow, and a trigger. In the vast majority of avalanche accidents, the slide is triggered by the person who's caught in it.

When I say "conditions," I don't just mean winter. There's this insidious misunderstanding, one I hear all the time, that the snowpack is inherently safer in the spring. I won't get into the mechanics of the spring snowpack here—this is a topic for much more science-minded folks than I am—but, generally, it's best to assume you can be caught in an avalanche anytime and anywhere there's snow on the ground.

One of the Colorado Front Range's most popular early- and late-season backcountry outings is St. Mary's Glacier, a permanent snowfield just outside the little hamlet of Alice. It's not great skiing (in fact, for much of the year, it's pretty bad skiing) but it's a short drive from Denver and it holds snow year-round, so diehards who want to ski every month often find themselves there for the bare-bones months of August and September. The wide slope up the snowfield itself is also relatively low angle and approachable, so people often ski or snowshoe there in the spring, when bluebird days abound.

That's what happened in early April 1998, when 38-year-old Tamara Sylvia Cohen lost her balance and slid down the slope. (She wasn't using skis or snowshoes.) As she stood up and began to head back up the slope toward her companion, Cohen triggered an avalanche, which fully buried her. Cohen and the friend she was hiking with were not equipped with rescue gear. Her companion searched frantically for her, and his shouts for help eventually attracted some other hikers to assist him.

The local sheriff's office got word of the accident after about 40 minutes, and SAR crews organized a speedy rescue effort thereafter, but it would be two hours before Cohen's body was recovered. We can't know for certain whether Cohen would have survived this accident if she and her companion had been equipped with beacons (her cause of death isn't specified in accident reports). But because they weren't, the odds were stacked against her.

Almost exactly one year later, a backcountry skier narrowly survived a near-miss accident in the same spot. It's a run I've skied dozens of times in conditions ranging from decent to abysmal, so this hits close to home.

The fact that these two accidents occurred so near one another, and that despite a recent fatality in the area, the survivor of the second avalanche wasn't carrying rescue equipment, is a good explanation as to why I'm writing this book. I don't want to keep reading nearly identical accident reports.

It should go without saying that the best way to survive an avalanche event is to avoid being involved in one in the first place. I know it sounds like I'm being coy. But think about it: Once the chain of events is set in motion, your odds of survival are drastically reduced at every turn. Better to arm yourself with as much information as you can and actively work to stay out of harm's way, no?

So—how to avoid an avalanche. Start by consulting people who are keeping very close track of the conditions. In areas where winter recreation is popular, there might be a daily avalanche bulletin (if you are unsure where to begin, head to the easy-to-remember avalanche.org, where you can find the advisory for your region).

If you read the day's avalanche forecast for the area you intend to ski, snowshoe, or otherwise recreate, you'll learn a few things right off the bat, and you don't need to know any complex snow science principles to start informing your decisions. An avalanche professional will have taken as much relevant information as possible—how much snow has fallen recently, what the weather and temperature are, their own observations from the field, what the snowpack has been like up to this point in the season—and used it to assign a danger level to the day's conditions. In North America, the danger runs on a five-point scale from Low (1) to Moderate to Considerable to High to Extreme (5).

Most accidents happen at Considerable danger. This makes sense, if you think about it: Most people know better than to go skiing or snowmobiling on High and Extreme days, and on Low and Moderate days, the conditions aren't as conducive to avalanches, so your odds of being caught are reduced. (That's not *always* the case; the 1998 St. Mary's accident occurred on a day with a Moderate forecast.)

The forecast might also tell you which slope aspects are best avoided—where winds have been depositing slabs of snow, for example—and how conditions might look different at 10,000 feet above sea level than they do at 7,500 feet.

Of course, if you leave the house without reading the avalanche forecast for the day, you don't know any of that. It takes just a few minutes to gather this information from the good people at your local avalanche center, and doing so can help you make important decisions about where (or where not) to travel. I cannot think of a legitimate reason not to equip yourself with this context.

Okay, so you've consulted the daily avalanche forecast and used it to narrow down your destination for the day's outing. Now, as you're packing your bag and coordinating meeting times with your partners, it's time for an important discussion: What's the plan, and most important, what are your limits?

Before you head into the winter backcountry, Spencer recommends "a very honest discussion with your partners about risk—and what is acceptable." This can be tricky because we don't always have the tools, skills, or language to communicate about that risk. We can always add to those tools by reading about past accidents and brushing up on our avalanche knowledge, but Spencer suggests also taking time to reflect on the days when it *seemed* like everything went right.

"Reflecting from the middle of my career on events that happened early in my career, I was underestimating the potential for avalanches, and overestimating my own understanding of what was going on," he says. "I was really fortunate that those were close calls—dramatic learning experiences—because they could easily have turned into events that killed me." Spencer says he recognized those close calls for what they were, even at the time, but that a lot of self-reflection comes days, months, even years after the fact.

That's how "Man, we spent way too much time in that gully last time we skied this run—let's check the map and see how we can avoid terrain traps tomorrow" and "I'm not up for a run that steep since the forecast is Considerable, especially since we saw shooting cracks that time; let's stick to the meadows today" make their way into our vocabularies. If you wouldn't be comfortable having a conversation like this with your partner(s), the time to think about why—and whether you should be heading into the backcountry with them at all—is before you hit the trail.

Next up in our choose-your-own-adventure scenario: what to bring.

Here's what it comes down to: When you are traveling in avalanche terrain, every single person in your party absolutely must carry a beacon, probe, *and* shovel. (Yes, all three!) I'm not going to go into great detail about how each item functions or which specific product is the best, because there are countless experts out there who can explain it much better than I can.* In the most basic terms, you need an avalanche transceiver (also called a beacon; say either, and people will know what you mean) to narrow down the burial location, a probe to pinpoint that location, and a shovel to dig someone out. If even one piece of that equipment is missing, you cannot effectively unbury a companion without a miraculous stroke of luck—and it is my understanding that luck favors the prepared.

---

* There are many excellent resources on the market for understanding what avalanche equipment is, how it functions, and how to keep yourself and your friends safe in avalanche terrain. For a primer, I recommend Bruce Tremper's *Avalanche Essentials*; when you think you're ready to try out for the varsity squad, pick up his *Staying Alive in Avalanche Terrain*.

Sometimes things fall apart because the victim(s) and their friends don't all have a beacon, probe, and shovel, or maybe they're equipped with one or two of those things but not all three. They don't know it yet, but their fates may have already been sealed by the lack of rescue gear they're carrying. Between 1996 and 2006, as modern digital beacons became increasingly commonplace, at least 208 avalanche incidents resulting in 220 fatalities took place. In 110 of those incidents—anywhere from 40 to a whopping 67 percent of the time, depending on the season—carrying no or inadequate rescue gear was identified as a contributing factor.

To me, this is the most terrifying possible outcome of what begins as a fun day in the snow: the utter helplessness of looking at a vast pile of blocky avalanche debris, knowing time is of the essence, and having no way to find your friend.

But after the slide, it's too late to equip yourself with the gear you need to find someone and pull them from the debris. The moment the snow fractures, what you're carrying is what you'll have to use—there's no going back. And because you don't know if or when that will happen, the moment your fate is sealed is really the moment you shut the car door and ski or hike away from the parking lot.

Beacon, probe, shovel—check. You've planned for the worst.

Once you arrive at the trailhead with the necessary gear in hand, the possible ways to find oneself buried in an avalanche are myriad. Maybe the slope looks safe, so you decide not to hassle with skiing one at a time. Maybe there's one short section of steeper slope just above a gully, and it's tantalizing to cross it so you can get to those meadows. Maybe you're just trailing along after a more experienced friend, who's taken an avalanche class and has never led you astray so far. Maybe you decide to take just one more lap, despite that the day is heating up and the snowpack is changing.

Whatever the reason, whatever combination of poor preparation and bad luck, no one starts their day expecting to be buried in an avalanche. Sometimes—rarely—it really is just a matter of being in the wrong place at the wrong time. And once you're buried, your companions are your best shot at getting out alive.

With about 15 minutes between burial and asphyxiation, the vast majority of avalanche victims barely have time for their companions to get to the site of their burial, find them, and dig them out. The chance that a SAR team can arrive on the scene and deploy rescue dogs to find someone before they expire is vanishingly small.

And that's if they survive the ride. About a quarter of those buried in avalanches are killed by trauma. When an avalanche breaks loose, it moves like liquid, and the river picks up branches and rocks and chunks of ice along with whoever's caught up in the melee. You're pinballing downhill as if you're being jostled around in a dryer. It's impossible to tell which way is up, let alone avoid whatever obstacles lie in your path.

If you make it down the slope without breaking your neck, you'll feel the river begin to slow down. If you've kept your wits about you, you'll carve out a little airspace. Like Dracula (or as if you're covering a sneeze), touch your shoulder with the opposite arm, carving out a little bubble of oxygen for your mouth and nose.

Then the concrete begins to harden, and you're in your memory-foam coffin. There are no more decisions to make. After the slide, you have to wait.

If you are traveling alone, you do not have this luxury. Another 27 avalanche victims killed between 1996 and 2006 were traveling solo. In December 1999, 25-year-old Michael Barrett ventured out alone to ski Quandary Peak, one of Colorado's more approachable Fourteeners. Its standard route avoids most of the peak's prime avalanche slopes, but no winter mountaineering is completely safe from slides.

In my early 20s, my then-boyfriend and I had the bright idea to snowshoe up Quandary Peak. Neither of us carried (or even knew about) rescue gear, and we were embarrassingly ill-equipped for a very cold day at altitude. We made it to tree line, where the wind howled and the snowpack settled violently under our snowshoes—a phenomenon I would later learn was called "whoomphing"—before throwing in the towel and heading back to Breckenridge for a beer. This would be one of the smartest decisions we made together during our partnership. (Five years later, I returned to Quandary in winter, this time equipped with knowledgeable partners and rescue gear. We didn't summit then, either; as is often the case, the wind-scoured upper slopes made for dicey conditions.)

When Barrett didn't show up for work a couple of days later, his coworkers became worried and reported him missing. Searchers eventually found him at around 13,400 feet elevation. He had died from massive trauma, caused by an avalanche that had carried him down a rocky gully. Barrett likely wouldn't have survived his ride regardless. But if he'd been traveling with a partner, even one with little knowledge of the winter backcountry, could that person have talked him into avoiding the dangerous gully?

You already know that backcountry skiers, splitboarders, snowshoers, and snowmobilers should always be equipped with an avalanche transceiver. By equipped, I mean wearing on your person; it doesn't do you any good if your beacon leads your friends to your backpack, which may well have been torn off on the ride down. When you leave the parking lot, everyone in the party turns their beacons on and checks to make sure they're working properly. At this point, everybody's beacons are in transmit mode—that is, they're transmitting a signal on a specific frequency.

If someone's caught in an avalanche, they don't have to do anything with their beacon. They have enough to worry about. Everyone else on the scene toggles a switch on their beacons, allowing them to receive the signal the now-victim is transmitting.

When someone's caught, that's often when their companions realize the gravity of not having adequate rescue gear. In February

2003, two young men set out to snowboard Hatch Peak, a popular spot in Hatcher Pass, the site of my practice burial for the SAR dogs. Anthony Watters, 24, was wearing his beacon and carried a probe and shovel, but his 18-year-old companion didn't have any rescue gear with him. When Watters triggered a slide from below, both young men were buried; the friend dug himself out but had no way to find Watters.

With no way to search, Watters's friend made his way to the Hatcher Pass Lodge. It would be 90 minutes before Watters was found. By then, he had passed away.

If, on the other hand, your friends are carrying beacons, know how to use them, and have practiced with them frequently, they can do a beacon search and find you pretty efficiently. Depending on the size of the slide and how big and difficult the debris field is to cross, they might manage it in just a few minutes.

Once your friends have honed in on your beacon's signal, they have to figure out where to dig. That's when the probe has its big moment. Like a giant tent pole, a collapsible probe is lightweight and easy to stuff in a backpack. Your friends will assemble their probes and jab at the snow, methodically spiraling outward from where your beacon has led them, until they feel it strike your squishy human form rather than the frozen ground. Eureka!

Now it's time to get you out. The snow is basically concrete, remember, not the loose, sugary stuff, so your companions can't just dig with their hands. They're assembling their shovels and teaming up to dig as quickly as possible. Time is running out.

If luck is on your side—if you didn't die on the way down and the slide didn't carry you too far and your friends reacted quickly and you managed to create an airspace—you've been buried for maybe 12 minutes now.

Finally, they see your jacket—not your face. They dig carefully to secure your airway and scoop some snow out of your mouth. You're looking pretty blue. That friend who's taken a first aid class thinks quickly and exposes enough of your chest to perform CPR. Fifteen minutes after the scariest ride of your life, you come to, grateful for your good taste in friends.

If that sounds like a lot of pressure to place on one's companions, good. It's a big responsibility. That scenario is textbook: Everything went right, and you got lucky at every turn. That's what things look like when the nightmare turns out alright. But, as dozens of people learn every winter in the United States, it doesn't always work out that way. And if you're traveling alone, you don't have the hope of solid friends to bail you out. Your story ends the moment you're buried.

I spend a lot of time thinking about how to avoid avalanches because I've spent so much time learning what happens after the slide—the immediate aftermath, when everything is in motion and speed is key, and also the days and months and years afterward, when things slow down and people have to learn to live without a loved one. What happens after the slide is one of the best reasons I can think of to avoid being caught in the first place.

The Alaska search dogs are fast, so I've probably been stuck in the cave less than 10 minutes by the time I hear the jingling of tags, though of course it feels infinitely longer. The dog—I can't yet tell which one it is—alerts above me. (Sometimes an alert means jumping on a handler or sitting down at the location of the buried victim; some dogs even alert differently for a live subject than one who's passed away.)

Soon, little white paws are digging at the surface. Someone with a shovel moves a few pieces of my cave away, and a friendly pink nose pokes through the hole. One of the duck tollers—a favorite breed for avalanche dogs up here—has found me and wiggles right up to bop me with his nose. His handler thrusts a well-loved dog toy into my mittened hands, and I crawl out of the cave into the dreary Alaskan December to reward this dog for getting me out of the snow. I am very glad not to have been buried in a real avalanche, and to this day, I'm doing everything I can to keep it that way.

LESSONS LEARNED

- **Avoid avalanches.** This absolutely doesn't mean avoiding the backcountry during the winter, although on High and Extreme days, it might mean skiing at the resort or getting some exercise on the flat, groomed trails near town, instead. It does mean knowing what constitutes avalanche terrain and avoiding it when conditions are conducive to slides. It means taking five minutes to read the local forecast not just on the days you go out, but every day throughout the season, which allows you to track and understand patterns. It's also crucial to practice good travel techniques: Ski one at a time, and use the same technique to cross steep slopes. Ski completely out of the reach of avalanche runout when you finish your run. Watch your companions closely when it's their turn, and should the unthinkable happen, keep watching—you'll need to know where to look for them. All this applies whether you're ripping gnarly lines or snowshoeing through meadows below steep slopes or bootpacking up a peak.

- **Get educated.** If you're going into the backcountry when there's snow on the ground, you need to take an avalanche class. If you're not quite ready to shell out for a pricey multiday class, you're still not off the hook. Gear shops and alpine clubs all over the country offer free and inexpensive classroom nights and lectures every season, and attending one of those, while not the same immersive experience as the standard three-day Recreational Level 1 course (strongly recommended if you'll be spending lots of time in the winter backcountry), is far better than nothing. You'll learn how to read and interpret an avalanche forecast and how to identify avalanche terrain, which are two of the most important skills for a novice winter traveler.

- **Carry all your rescue gear every time—and know how to use it.** You already know that it's crucial to carry a beacon, probe, and shovel every time you go out. Once you own the requisite gear, you'll need to practice with it regularly in order to be ready to use it if the worst-case scenario comes to pass. You'll also need to do maintenance on your gear, like taking the batteries out of your beacon at the end of the season or after a particularly wet tour so they don't corrode and replacing them regularly with fresh ones. Even if you're just going for a "short tour" or the danger is rated Low or Moderate, don't leave home without all three pieces of rescue gear. Is any convenience worth being caught without it if today's the day you really need it?

- **Demand that your partners do the same.** If, like me, you struggle to be assertive, it can be tough to demand that friends do anything. But despite my nearly pathological need for people to like me, I have a hard line here: I won't backcountry ski with anyone who doesn't carry and know how to operate a beacon, probe, and shovel, and I'm reticent to tour with anyone who doesn't hold at least a Recreational Level 1 certification. This rule might sound melodramatic, but this is literally life and death we're talking about. If I'm buried in a slide, do I really want my only companion to be someone who's never taken a class and doesn't know what to do? No way. I want it to be my husband, who I know is incredibly cool under pressure. Or the friend of a friend I know who dug his companion out after an avalanche, then promptly threw up because he'd worked himself to the point of exhaustion. Or my mentor, Eeva, who can find and flag three buried victims in just a couple of minutes. The point is, I choose my friends care-fully, and my ski partners even more so. There are plenty of people I'll happily rip laps with at the resort, but I'm squirrelly about who I'll ski the backcountry with. I hereby bestow you with the power to do the same. You, too, can apply extremely high standards to your ski partners.

- **Don't travel alone.** In all the scenarios I mentioned in this chapter, most have at least a small margin for error. If you ski in avalanche-prone terrain on a High danger day (don't do this!), I suppose you *could* get lucky—there's no guarantee you'll be caught. If you forget your beacon at home or don't turn it on (don't do this, either), or if your friends don't have a probe or a shovel (make sure they do), there's a non-zero chance they'll hit the jackpot, maybe see your gloved hand sticking out of the snow, and find you anyway. I don't rec-ommend any of this, obviously, but you see my point: With almost any mistake you might make in the backcountry, there is a teeny, tiny margin for error. But that's not the case when you're traveling alone. Venturing out solo can be an incredible, empowering experience. But it comes with a steep price tag. It reduces your margin for error to exactly zero. Any of the dozens of other possible little mistakes you might make equals certain death. To me, that's not worth it, which is why if I can't find a partner, I'm skiing the resort or stick-ing to the Nordic trails.

Chapter Eight

Disappointment on the DC

FOR A FEW SHORT MOMENTS AFTER THE SUN SLIPS AWAY FOR good, it is utterly, completely black. It's the kind of inky darkness where you can't see your hand right in front of your face. Our three headlamps, ambling up the snowfield between Paradise and Camp Muir, appear to be the only sources of light on the mountain, maybe in the whole park. Eventually, what passes for the moon—a pale sliver of waxing crescent—faintly illuminates the slope above me, or maybe it's just my eyes adjusting.

I don't mind the darkness. Somehow, it makes the distance between our car and 10,000-foot Camp Muir feel a little easier: I can't see each step I'm putting in, so maybe I won't feel them later, either.

Just before 11:00 p.m., we crest a little bench on the snowfield and spot the twinkling lights of Muir, the most formal stopover between the trailhead and the summit of Mount Rainier.* I feel a rush of excitement, which is immediately tempered by perspective: Muir still looks impossibly far away, beyond that is the most difficult part of the climb, and I'm already feeling the effects of climbing for five or six straight hours.

"We'll be there in 20," Bix says confidently, stopping short behind me. I am buoyed and also slightly annoyed by his cheery

---

* Tahoma, in the language of the Puyallup people.

estimation. How is this so easy for him? Our friend Daniel is a few paces behind, looking more chipper than I feel.

Twenty minutes of one foot in front of the other, I tell myself. *Easy.*

Bix's guess is right on the money. Twenty minutes later, we arrive at Muir, drop our packs, and start pulling out layers. Soon, the three of us are snuggled together under a single zero-degree sleeping bag. We'll bivouac here for a couple of fitful hours—not quite sleeping, not fully awake—then start the climb as the guided parties start to stir in their tents.

Camp Muir is often sandwiched between two thick slices of cloud cover, but tonight, the night sky is on full display. The Milky Way streams across my entire field of vision. I think about how cold it is in space, billions of miles away, on the stars that make up my favorite constellation, Cassiopeia. A shooting star appears, its presence fleeting, reminding me that I, too, am spinning through the universe at a thousand miles an hour.

The downside to having no cloud cover is that it's very cold—in the single digits Fahrenheit. My hands and face are grateful when the alarm on Bix's watch goes off at 1:00 a.m. I'm not quite rested, per se, but I'm definitely tired of sitting still. We stuff our layers back into our backpacks and don our crampons, each of us on our own planets, thinking about the climb ahead. The three of us walk to the edge of Camp Muir and rope up.

A few guided parties have already begun their climbs. They illuminate the route with bobbing orbs of white light, rendering the mountain a life-sized diorama, a caricature of itself, just like the one at the Longmire Visitor Center, 6,000 feet below.

Bix, Daniel, and I have set out to climb the Disappointment Cleaver (often called the DC, for short), which is by far the most popular and least technical route on Mount Rainier. The National Park Service (NPS) estimates that 75 percent of all Rainier climbs are via the

DC. It's also a typical descent route, given its relative lack of objective hazards, compared to the nearly 60 other routes on the peak.

Entire books have been written about Mount Rainier and its historic climbs, but there's less readily available information about the history of the DC, specifically. The "Cleaver" part of its name is distinctly Pacific Northwestern, but the "Disappointment" is less clear. The Park asserts that Ingraham Glacier saw its first known ascent in 1885, by A. L. Brown and a group from the Yakima Tribe. The route from the top of Ingraham Glacier to the summit—the DC—began to gain popularity after the Gibraltar Ledges route, traditional until then, collapsed in 1936.

Mount Rainier is 14,410 feet above sea level, but its elevation alone is a poor description of its mass. It's much closer to sea level than the Colorado Fourteeners, which typically rise something like 3,000 feet from the trailhead, meaning its prominence (a measure of how tall a summit stands independent of any other nearby peak) is a whopping 13,212 feet. It is the most heavily glaciated peak in the Lower 48. It's also considered by scientists to be among the planet's most dangerous volcanoes, thanks to its potential to produce deep, fast-flowing rivers of mud and debris that could wipe out the entire Puyallup Valley, but that's a story for another time.

It's so big, in fact, that in December 1946, a twin-engine C-47 plane with 32 marines aboard, en route from San Diego to Seattle, was caught in a storm and vanished on the side of the mountain. Five feet of snow fell at the 9,500-foot elevation over the next three days. Despite repeated search efforts by then–Assistant Chief Ranger Bill Butler, the plane and its passengers weren't found for another eight months. (For his efforts in finding the plane and the marines, Butler was awarded the Distinguished Public Service Certificate, the navy's highest civilian honor, and the Department of the Interior's Distinguished Service Medal.) Only 11 of the bodies were found, and none has ever been recovered, thanks to near-constant rockfall. All 32 passengers are presumed to remain at 10,500 feet on the South Tahoma Glacier.

It's a vast, unforgiving landscape if you're flying a plane in a storm, but it's not exactly a walk in the park if you're on the ground, either. As we trudge across the Ingraham Flats, I can't help but think about one of the worst accidents in American mountaineering history. In June 1981, a group of 6 guides and 23 clients set out from Camp Muir toward the summit via the Disappointment Cleaver route. Ninety minutes or so from camp, three clients decided they couldn't continue, and one of the guides turned around with them to deliver them to Muir.

The rest continued upward, and not far from where I'm standing, three respected guides—John Day, Mike Targett, and Peter Whittaker—took a break to assess the conditions. They weren't good, thanks to the exposed slope above, and the guides knew their clients didn't have the experience to make good time through the exposed runout. No one had made the summit for an entire week beforehand, and this wasn't going to be the day the streak was broken; the guides turned everyone around.

But it was already too late. According to the report published in the 1982 edition of *Accidents in North American Mountaineering*,[*] the American Alpine Club's annual review and analysis of the previous year's climbing accidents:

> Apparently, a very large serac or ice formation toppled over or let go about 800 vertical feet above the waiting climbers. This ice formation broke into several massive ice blocks which crashed rapidly down the slope and created an unusually large snow and ice avalanche.

---

[*] The American Alpine Club has published this collection annually since 1948. Beginning in 2016, the publication was renamed *Accidents in North American Climbing* to better reflect the makeup of its contents; the AAC still publishes a mix of mountaineering and climbing accident reports and analyses.

The guides shouted at the group to run, but "most of them were unable to get clear before the snow and ice was upon them." When the debris came to rest, it was 75 feet deep—a completely unsurvivable depth. The eleven climbers killed that day have never been recovered.

This wasn't the only, or even the most recent, huge accident to take place on Rainier. In June 1998, an avalanche swept two rope teams—a total of 10 climbers—off the DC. The situation was incredibly complex, involving steep, icy slopes, vertical rock bands, continued avalanche potential, and a 300-foot drop to the glacier below. Some of the stranded climbers clung to the edge of a cliff, their rope tangled in the rocky terrain, while a group below them dangled precariously. One climber, stuck even lower, was exposed to constant frigid snowmelt and died as a result. Thanks to a daring rescue by NPS personnel (including climbing ranger Mike Gauthier, who heard the announcement on his radio while at the summit and snowboarded down to the scene of the accident), along with private and army helicopters, the other nine climbers involved were rescued.

Knowing all this—and having read Gauthier's report in the following year's edition of *Accidents*, in which he notes that this area of the route is notorious for rock and icefall—I'm acutely aware that to climb this mountain is a serious undertaking. I haven't approached training lightly. For months, we've been hiking the trails near our dingy apartment in Golden, Colorado, with increasingly heavy packs, eventually graduating to a couple of Front Range Fourteeners to train at altitude. By the time we set out from our car the evening before, I was the strongest I'd been in years, maybe ever.

I've spent plenty of time on glaciers and have peered into the maw of more than one seemingly bottomless crevasse. Still, the gravity of our climb doesn't truly dawn on me until we're about an hour out of Camp Muir. We've reached the first bottleneck on the route: a crevasse about the width of a sidewalk. A mangled two-by-four, riddled with crampon holes, stretches across the crack in the glacier.

Crevasses don't just appear in the snow to swallow whole parties of climbers alive. Picture a Snickers bar. If you unwrap it and set it on the table in front of you, the chocolate coating is smooth and featureless. But if you bend it in half, the chocolate cracks, exposing peanuts and nougaty goodness. Glaciers are basically the same, minus the caramel filling. They are enormous, slow-moving rivers of ice, traveling inexorably downhill; moving at a "glacial pace" means you're taking a few millennia to let gravity pull you from Point A to Point B. When this mass of ice loses elevation or turns a corner, cracks—crevasses—open up. Sometimes they're big enough to envelop a car. Sometimes they're covered by a thin snowbridge, which conceals them from view but can't withstand the weight of, say, a climber wearing a pack filled with mountaineering equipment.

This section of the route isn't the most heavily crevassed on the mountain, but it's given climbers its share of trouble. In 1989, a park ranger and her partner were roped together as they descended the DC route. A snowbridge collapsed beneath one of them, pulling them both in. Fortunately, after digging themselves out from under fallen blocks of ice, they discovered a ramp and were able to climb it back to the surface. The ranger was a little banged up but otherwise fine, and her partner was uninjured; both were evacuated by helicopter later that afternoon.

Of course, it's far from guaranteed that you'll land safely on a solid ramp and be able to walk back up to the surface, so glacier travel requires very much probing, occasional backtracking, and perpetual readiness to self-arrest.

I have more mountaineering experience than Bix or Daniel, so I'm in the lead. I consider the length of wood frozen in place at my feet. It's a poor substitute for those ladders you see lashed together through the Khumbu Icefall on Mount Everest, which at least have the advantage of looking very adventuresome.

"Everything OK up there?" Bix wants to know.

"Yep, just keep me on a tight belay here," I tell him, not relishing the idea of needing to be pulled out of this crevasse. I still have the benefit of darkness, which means it's a little easier to ignore how deep this thing is.

The two-by-four is steadier than I'd expected. I reach the other side unscathed and turn to watch Bix and Daniel cross. I'm much more worried about this part—not because I don't think they're capable, but because if something goes wrong, I'll be the one tasked with setting up an anchor and rigging a pulley system to haul them out. I know how to do it and I'm pretty strong, but the fact of the matter is that, with a pack on, each of them probably has at least 70 pounds on me.

Bix and Daniel each make it across without incident. Now we have to wind our way through the maze of crevasses between us and the Disappointment Cleaver.

It's still dark when we reach the base of the DC. Daniel hasn't said much for a while, but I've been caught up in my own reverie and haven't noticed. Now he wants to stop for a bite.

"We can't stop here," I tell him. Unlike the rest of the route, whose chunks of volcanic rock are held in place by ice and snow, the DC is bare rock and scree. (The stretch from Ingraham Flats to the DC is known colloquially as the Bowling Alley, if that tells you anything about the frequency of rockfall.) We're wearing climbing helmets, which are specifically engineered to protect our brains from rock falling from above, but those can only do so much—they're good for a softball, *maybe,* but not a microwave, and certainly nothing bigger. Strictly speaking, there's no "safe" way to climb the DC, but the closest substitute for safety is to climb it quickly. This means no lollygagging, and certainly no stopping for a break.

It also means we have to adjust the configuration of our rope. When traveling across glaciated terrain, we leave a much longer length of rope between each member of our party. This allows us to spread out our weight, helps us belay one another across crevasses, and gives us some rope to work with should we need to set up a pulley system in case of a crevasse fall. Now we're out of crevasse danger for the time being, and if we don't shorten up the rope between us, it's practically guaranteed to snag on rocks or, worse, knock rocks loose and send them flying down the DC at anyone below us.

Rockfall tends to be worse during the daytime, when the sun has loosened the ice that normally grips rocks in place. But it's not entirely unheard of for rocks to kick loose even during the chill of the night. That happened in 1985, when spontaneous rockfall from the Cathedral Rocks Gap came showering down just after 1:00 a.m. and an ascending climber was "struck on the left side of the torso area by a one meter square boulder, and then fell ten meters down a scree gully." Another party helped the injured climber back to Muir. And while the danger is most acute in this rocky section, there's still a chance of rockfall between the DC and the summit: In 2001, a football-size rock struck a climber in the abdomen just above the DC.

It occurs to me that there are probably countless other less serious rockfall incidents involving slightly smaller rocks that simply haven't been reported in the years since these close calls. I swallow hard, thinking that a boulder half the size of a square meter—a football, even!—can still do plenty of damage.

As the leader of our team, it's my job to navigate. I hadn't anticipated any trouble with this; I've navigated many off-trail miles, including my share in the dark. Plus, this route is what guides call the "trade route," meaning it sees hundreds of ascents every season. It's pretty easy to follow a trail when it's the only packed-down snow in sight. But in September, previous months of sun and relatively warm temperatures means there's no snow on the Disappointment Cleaver.

I'm on the route—I'm certain of this because the DC, though one of the steepest slopes on the entire route, is never more difficult than third- or fourth-class scrambling, so if the climbing gets more technical than that, I'll know to stop and reassess. Still, I'm having to keep my wits about me. It helps that the guide services, as they typically do, have wanded the route. Every now and then, the glint of my headlamp catches a piece of reflective tape attached to a bamboo wand, assuring me that I'm where I'm supposed to be.

In early September 1997, right around the time of year we're climbing, a pair of climbers set out from their 11,000-foot camp for the summit via the DC. Despite having been warned at the ranger station that recent storms had left parts of the usual boot track covered in snow, they left most of their gear at camp. "Poor weather had been predicted and other parties reported seeing them head into the clouds earlier that morning," reads the *Accidents* report. Still, the party carried only fanny packs—no map, compass, wands, or even gear to bivouac, should the need arise. When another whiteout kicked up just 1,800 vertical feet above their camp, the party became disoriented, "unable to find their way up or down the mountain." In a very lucky cell phone call, the party managed to make contact with the ranger station and requested a rescue; the weather cleared three hours later and rangers were able to escort the climbers back to their camp.

On the morning of our climb, the weather is perfect. In a whiteout, or even in strong winds or thick clouds, both of which regularly set in with or without warning on Rainier, these wands would be tough to see. I'm equipped with a detailed topo map and a compass, but this is not a place I want to test my mettle with dead reckoning.

In my life, I have witnessed a handful of truly memorable sunrises. The one that greets us at the top of the Disappointment Cleaver that September morning blows them all away, almost defying description. It's a combination of things, I guess—unless you're socked in, the view from the top of the DC is truly spectacular. You can see the edge of the summit crater, 2,100 vertical feet above, and the world stretches out beneath you, as if you're flying in a plane. The soft, peachy light warms my face, allowing me to enjoy the relief of being out of rockfall danger, if only momentarily.

The sunrise that morning is also bookmarked in my memory because, though I didn't know it at the time, my grandfather had passed away just hours earlier. He'd spent much of my childhood scaring me into eating my vegetables so a monster he called the boo-rang wouldn't get me. As I'd grown up and started to under-stand his odd, dry sense of humor, something clicked. He liked to know where I was going so he could keep an eye on the weather there. I always sent him a postcard.

This is the often-overlooked cost of spending time in remote places where you cannot be reached. When I was on my first backpacking trip, a monthlong course with the National Outdoor Leadership School when I was 21, my parents had to put my childhood dog to sleep. He was very old and I should have seen it coming, but it was such a shock to realize it had actually happened. I have a tendency to mentally catalog every possible catastrophic outcome, but more often than not, I come out of the field and everything's fine. When that's not the case, despite my theoretical preparation, it's jarring.

I knew my grandpa wasn't well. The week before, I'd visited him in the hospital. He was in and out of consciousness, occasionally making a joke about whatever was on the TV but mostly sleeping. His doctor had been insisting he wear oxygen for his COPD for a few years, and while my grandpa had initially resisted, he could no longer get by without it. That, and being able to do less and less of his own yard work—difficult for a man who was stoic to a fault—meant I knew the end of his life wasn't far off.

I talked about postponing the Rainier climb, but my mom, a former emergency room nurse, didn't figure his death was imminent and encouraged me to stick to our plans. I knew, too, that he'd be annoyed if I skipped the climb I'd talked about for months to sit at his bedside and worry. He'd just want to know what the weather was like. I'd send him a postcard when I got back down to the visitor center.

I thought about my grandfather a lot as I climbed the DC that night. More important than instilling wilderness skills or teaching me to tie knots, he'd taught me the importance of a strong work ethic. He worked for IBM, the computer company, his entire career. He didn't last long in retirement, almost immediately volunteering to ride along with the detectives at the local police department, where he ended up logging eight-hour days, five days a week, for another 20 years without ever collecting a dime.

We weren't exactly close until I was a teenager (though even then, he could never resist an opportunity to ask me how much my torn-up jeans had cost). When my mom told him I'd gotten a job at the local pet food store at 16, he called to congratulate me. I'm told he often bragged to his friends and the detectives at the Longmont Police Department that his granddaughter usually had two or three jobs. (This was really the result of an inability to commit, paired with what my other granddad would call "champagne taste on a beer budget," but I'll take it.) When you earn the admiration of someone whose response to a straight-A report card is typically "Not bad," followed by a change in subject, it feels like a real accomplishment—and working hard, with him, was how you did it.

As it turns out, a strong work ethic is a crucial component of mountaineering, which is really just a glamorous-sounding word for moving slowly uphill while not feeling very well. And that's exactly what I did on the DC: I put one foot in front of the other, moving slowly and without any particular grace but steadily all the same, blissfully unaware of the fact that my grandfather wouldn't be around to read my postcard this time.

It sounds silly, but I hadn't realized just how long an early September night on the side of an icy peak would feel. By the time the first rays of sunlight begin to appear, framing the distant summits of other Cascade volcanoes in a fluffy stratus sea, I'm questioning our decision to climb Rainier in a single push. Setting out from Daniel's car, to say nothing of our departure from his Seattle apartment, feels eons ago.

I'm not the only one feeling the effects of our effort and the altitude. Daniel (who, funnily enough, we often call by his initials, DC) is usually chipper if a little sardonic, but as the light intensifies, I can see that he's looking pretty green around the gills. At first, I'll admit, I'm a little annoyed. We've been training for this climb for months and planning it for even longer, and what, he's tired? We're all tired! I want to grab his shoulders and shake him: *Why didn't you train harder?*

Bix and I share a sidelong glance. Daniel has slowed down considerably over the last hour, and when he does say something, it's a little slurred. When he drops his pack on the ground and collapses in a heap on top of it without so much as pulling out a water bottle or a snack, I take a closer look at him. He's pale, and his eyes are sunken behind big, dark circles. He's not just tired. He's got acute mountain sickness (see chapter 2 for a more in-depth account of AMS signs and symptoms).

AMS isn't just a problem on the high peaks of the Himalayas; signs and symptoms regularly occur when, say, visiting skiers land at Denver International Airport and head up to 10,000 feet above sea level later that day. Here, at 12,300 feet, it's not all that surprising that Daniel has been transformed into a cartoon character I'd call "Mr. Malaise." He's not alone. One group needed a hand from climbing rangers in 2001, when all three of their party was felled by AMS and dehydration; after taking on some fluids, they were escorted back to Camp Muir.

It's not just inexperienced climbers who find themselves felled by altitude illness on Mount Rainier. In 1995, a group of three volunteers summited the volcano and planned to be the last party down the mountain, descending via the DC, so they could help search for some overdue climbers who'd gone up via Liberty Ridge. Eventually, they encountered another team they'd first met on the summit, one member of which suspected he was suffering from cerebral edema. (He happened to be a doctor, so his assessment is relatively reliable.) Intermittently disoriented and vomiting, this climber was in bad shape, though his condition improved as the volunteers helped him make his way down the mountain. By the time they reached Ingraham Flats, the climber thought he'd improved, though he was still unable to recognize the knots used to tie into the rope, which must have been familiar to him under normal circumstances. Eventually, he was able to make it off the mountain on his own from Pebble Creek, below Camp Muir. The entire incident sounds like a terrifying couple of hours, and I'm eager to avoid a similar ordeal today.

Daniel's feeling pretty crappy, so I'm assessing whether I think he can make it back down under his own power. It's a good sign that he's coherent enough to wish us a happy anniversary—Bix and I planned this climb to celebrate our first wedding anniversary, which now feels somewhat beside the point—and even snap a photo of us looking cold and tired.

"You should go up and finish it without me," he offers. I don't doubt that he means it, but I'm sure as hell not leaving him here, exposed and maybe too exhausted to take care of himself, at the top of the DC. I want to summit—badly, even—but if my first year of marriage has taught me anything, it's that the destination is a sort of nebulous, intangible thing, but the journey to get there (and how you treat your partner along the way) matters a lot more. A little corny, maybe, but very much my mindset as I run through a mental checklist of my friend's condition.

"No way, dude," Bix says before I have a chance to answer. "We started this climb together, and we're gonna stay together." I married a good one.

With the pressure of summiting off the table, we linger at the top of the DC. We take in the view—how often will we get to take in a sunrise like this? Bix pulls out our little Jetboil stove and makes Daniel some noodles. With some salty calories and fluid on board, he rallies, ready for the very long journey back to Paradise.

Unsurprisingly, a great many mountaineering accidents happen on the descent, when climbers are spent and nerves are frayed. It's impossible to know for certain how often this happens, given a lack of reporting and the countless climbable peaks on the planet, but it's a lot: A study published in 2017 analyzed 5,368 accidents in the Austrian Alps over a nine-year period and found that just over three-quarters of them occurred during descent from the summit.

This possibility is on my mind as the three of us start down the steep, rocky slopes of the DC, which is essentially covered in tiny ball bearings. Daniel's a little better than he was 45 minutes ago, but his crampon-clad feet still feel like lead, and he trips more than once. Normally, we'd ditch the rope and each move at our own pace until we got back to the Ingraham Glacier, but given the sheer drop-off below, it makes sense to keep a closer eye on grumbly Daniel. (For years after this, I will tease him mercilessly for his snippy correction of my pronunciation of "Ingraham," which he swears not to remember. Sorry, D.)

By the time we arrive back at the crevasse with the two-by-four, the sun is fully up and the snow has started to soften. This means it's time to hurry, since melting snow means rocks will become dislodged from the ice to career down on us. The two-by-four is gone, not that it would do much good now that it's not frozen in place, and we have to hop across the crevasse.

The descent from Camp Muir back to Paradise is nothing short of grueling, thanks to the now-hot sun and my tired quads. When we arrive back to the car, except for our short breaks at Muir and the top of the DC, we've been moving for 22 hours. Later, at Daniel's place in Ballard, I'll turn on my phone and get a voice-mail I don't want to hear from my mom. We'll put away two large consolation-prize pizzas and sleep for 10 hours.

But right now, as I drop my pack on the pavement, crack open a beer, and toast with two of my favorite people, I'm not thinking about any of that. I'm just proud of my effort and very, very tired.

LESSONS LEARNED

- **Start small. Don't get in over your head.** This book is not intended to be a resource for training for mountaineering. Lots of people know a lot more than I do about how to do this properly (I used Steve House's excellent resource *Training for the New Alpinism* to prepare for this climb). But it's not just about being fit. You could be an Olympic athlete and still not be prepared to climb a glaciated peak; it takes skills, too. For that reason, the National Park Service recommends climbing glaciated routes on smaller, lower-consequence peaks (Mount Saint Helens, Mount Hood, Mount Baker) before attempting DC. Many reputable outfitters offer courses in glacier travel and crevasse rescue, and some do this as part of a guided climb of one of the aforementioned volcanoes. If you're short on glacier travel experience and don't have an experienced friend who can mentor you, this is the route I suggest. This is not the place to muddle through after reading a couple of books and watching some YouTube videos. In other words, hopefully you don't need to rescue a partner from a crevasse—but if you do, you'd better be very certain you're doing it right.

- **Research the route.** By the time we started our climb, I'd been researching and training for about six months. I'm glad I knew what to expect. The DC is a relatively straightforward route, but as is illustrated in this chapter, there are still plenty of opportunities to get lost or off-route, especially if weather crops up. If you've researched enough to know a section maxes out at third- or fourth-class scrambling, but you are suddenly having to make fifth-class moves, you're a step ahead—you can stop and think before you find yourself cliffed out. Thanks to its popularity, the DC is convenient to research; there's an incredibly detailed official route description, climbers discuss it ad nauseum online, and it's mentioned in a handful of guidebooks. If information on the route you plan to climb isn't readily available, there are still plenty of ways to find out more, from calling the local ranger district to poring over topo maps to asking for beta online or at your local rock gym.

- **Pick a solid team.** Who you're climbing with matters even more when you're roped together. My approach to glacier travel is much like my approach to skiing in avalanche terrain, and, in fact, they often intersect. If something goes wrong, can I trust this person to keep a level head and solve the problem? I have lots of friends I love dearly but would never tie into a rope with. This is also a climb I wouldn't consider doing solo. Plenty of people have pulled this off—climbing rangers manage it countless times every season, for example, though they know the route inside and out—but, personally, it's beyond my risk tolerance to climb on a glacier without a partner who can pull me out of a crevasse. Bix and Daniel were trustworthy partners and the three of us had done plenty of trips together by the time we attempted Rainier—backpacking excursions, a weeklong rock climbing road trip, cross-country skiing in Alaska—but I wish we'd done a smaller, less committing route together to work out the kinks first.

- **The mountain will always be there.** It takes guts to turn around—often more than it would to simply trudge ahead. You've worked hard, you've come all this way, maybe you can see the summit. These feelings only increase with the challenge and size of the route. But errors can cascade, too—maybe you choose to go light and skip a spare pair of socks. This is nothing, but then you misstep on the approach hike and get your feet wet in a stream. No big deal, until you decide to push on despite signs of worsening weather. Things can escalate quickly on the mountain, and if you're facing the notion of spending an unplanned night exposed on the slopes of Mount Rainier, your frostbitten toes are suddenly going to be really sorry you didn't pack those socks or turn around when your feet got wet. I'm not suggesting every climb requires a complete change of clothes or that you should always turn around if your feet get wet. But they're things to keep in mind—every risk you accept should be on a growing mental list when it's time to make your next decision, because every choice you make affects the next. And in the end, the mountain will be there next month or next season or in five years. The question you need to ask yourself is: *Will you?*

- **Don't split up.** From day hikes of the Colorado Fourteeners to climbs of Mount Rainier to Mount Everest expeditions, there are countless stories of parties who split up, never to be reunited. It's usually some version of this: A group sets out. Partway up the peak, someone decides that for whatever reason, they can't go on. The group talks and decides that person will wait where they are or turn around and head back. They make a plan: The rest of the party will head up, quickly now that they don't have to wait for the lagging group member, and tag the summit. Then everyone will meet back up right here in this very spot, or maybe at the trailhead. Everyone will high-five. The problem is that very frequently it doesn't turn out that way because so many things can go wrong in the interim. The person who turned around takes a wrong turn and gets lost on the way down. The summit party lingers on top or takes a shortcut that misses the agreed-upon spot. At best, a missed connection can mean someone's sitting around at altitude, tired and annoyed, for a few extra hours. At worst, things can cascade until the situation is life or death. Your best bet is to stick together, even if it means not summiting.

CHAPTER NINE

It's a Dry Heat

THE BEST COFFEE MUG IN MY CABINET FEATURES A FULLY DRESSED cartoon skeleton surrounded by cacti and cow skulls. A smiling sun beats down on the red cliffs in the background; a nearby sign indicates that it's three miles to nowhere. Curly red letters inside the mug specify that it's a product of Arizona. The skeleton's shirt reads, "But it's a dry heat."

I'm a sucker for a good mug—the shelves above my coffee-maker are brimming with them, to the point that my husband has put a moratorium on new acquisitions until I'm willing to part with a few of our current collection, which I am not—but this is among my favorites. I am a product of the American West and have absolutely no tolerance for humidity. If it's 100 degrees outside, by all means, I'd rather crumble into dust and blow away than melt into a puddle on some damp coast. Also, I love a touch of the absurd.

I often think of this mug when I wake up in the desert. Usually, there is a fine layer of reddish dust coating my teeth, and I am forced to reckon with the idea that I might finally be making my long-awaited transformation into an actual pile of dust. As I'm taking stock of the dust in every crevice, it will dawn on me that, despite that the sun is barely overhead, it's already hot.

But it's a dry heat.

My early introduction to the wilderness was in environments of the other extreme. By the time I made my first extended forays into the desert, I'd endured painfully cold, sleepless nights, periods of 10 or 20 degrees below zero where I couldn't seem to eat enough to keep warm, even a bout of mild frostbite and the resulting purple tissue and lost toenails. I'd traversed vast swaths of inhospitable winter wilderness. They were deserts in every sense—dry, barren, desolate—except the heat. Surely, being too cold was harder and more dangerous than being too hot.

The thing is, heat—even the dry heat I prefer—can be pretty dangerous, too. We are fragile creatures, humans. Temperatures too far in either extreme can cause the human body to shut down. It starts with dizziness, tunnel vision, vertigo. You feel sweaty and weak, maybe a little nauseous. You might faint. Cramps and muscle spasms might be next, and eventually, delirium sets in. When the body temperature reaches 104 degrees Fahrenheit, things are dire—and in places where summer temperatures might easily top 110 degrees, this doesn't sound like much of a stretch.

Bix and I got married in September. We chose Labor Day weekend in part because it would be easier for our friends to take the time off to come out to Colorado for our wedding, and because it meant we could honeymoon in the desert without turning into the skeleton on my coffee mug.

A week after our wedding, we packed up the car and pointed it toward Moab. Some of our favorite memories together were in southeast Utah: a spring backpacking trip through Island in the Sky here, a Sunday afternoon spent exploring the infinite hallways and vestibules of the Fiery Furnace there.

First, we spent a few nights at a fancy lodge up the River Road (thanks, Mom and Dad). Almost immediately, I learned that strangers would send drinks over if I casually mentioned we were on our honeymoon. Bix found a channel that played *Butch Cassidy and the Sundance Kid* on a continuous loop and insisted on watching it every night of our stay. When in Rome, I guess.

Then, as much as I regretted leaving the free-flowing glasses of wine behind, we picked up a canoe and set out for five days on the Green River, which we planned to float for 47 miles through Labyrinth Canyon.

By early fall, the soaring desert temperatures had started to cool off from their triple-digit peak, but as we loaded our canoe and got ready to shove off from Ruby Ranch, it was in the mid-90s. I wore a long-sleeved cotton button-up shirt from the thrift store, a pair of baggy, lightweight linen pants (these would finish the trip with several red wine stains), a wide-brimmed hat like the one your grandmother wears to weed her garden, and enough high-SPF sunscreen to coat a small pachyderm. You know, your standard sexy honeymoon outfit.

We spent most of that first day chasing the fleeting patches of shade provided by the towering canyon walls. A few hours later, when we found a dusty campsite nine miles downstream, just beyond Trin-Alcove, I was soaked in sweat and extremely ready to peel out of my moist clothes and maybe even take a dip in the murky river.

We kicked aside a smattering of cow pies to make room for our tent, and I shimmied out of my shirt to rinse it off. As I wrung out the now-salty water, a handful of stand-up paddleboarders appeared at the bend just upstream. They moved quickly, even on the lazy current, but not so fast that I didn't catch a glimpse of a hatless, extremely sunburned woman in a polka-dot swimsuit. She spotted us and waved enthusiastically, revealing her pale underarm skin, which contrasted starkly with her reddened shoulders. *Oh man, I thought, she doesn't even know yet.*

A nasty sunburn like the one this unfortunate woman had alone isn't enough to kill you, but it's certainly miserable. She'd probably applied sunscreen that morning, but a single layer of SPF isn't enough to protect you for more than a few hours in the full bore of the desert sun. Long sleeves, on the other hand—while much less cute and considerably stinkier, particularly if you pair them with salty pit stains like the ones I'd been rocking—will keep the sun off all day.

We waved back, figuring she had a bit longer to enjoy the golden hour before she realized the state of her skin and had to start bribing her companions for aloe lotion.

Despite my self-satisfaction about my choice to cover up as much skin as possible, I woke up the next morning to an odd sensation inside my nose. I stuck a finger in there to investigate (don't judge me! I know you do this, too) and pulled out a perfect replica of my nostril: The sun's reflection off the water had sunburned the inside of my nose, which was now peeling. My body is a wonderland! Fortunately, Bix was already married to me, hence the trip we now found ourselves on, so I didn't have to put on any airs.

Now that I'd extracted my nose sculpture, I donned my Halloween costume ("vampire woman who must keep out of sun"), which was salty enough to basically stand up on its own, and slathered sunscreen on all remaining exposed skin, including up my nose. Then it was time to strike the tent and get ready for another very warm day on the water.

Speaking of water: It is what defines the desert. We think of deserts as these waterless places—that's the whole thing about them, right?—but in fact, water is in constant ebb and flow, its presence or absence defining these seemingly barren places in ways we often don't even see. The sandstone canyon walls exist because water has eroded its winding way through them over millions of years. Everything here, from river to rim, is equipped to make do with as little water as possible: delicate clusters of cryptobiotic soil, skittering lizards, hardy desert bighorns.

The desert is a tempestuous landscape. Sometimes this is understated: It's a slow burn, with its poisonous creatures and high temperatures, but it's wild, turbulent, unwieldable. And when the water does come, it really comes.

For three days, we dutifully drank the now-hot clean water we'd brought along, one Nalgene liter at a time. We'd brought two five-gallon jugs of water, and the first had gone pretty quickly. On the fourth morning, as I hauled the remaining plastic water jug over to our canoe, it occurred to me that it was very much lighter. I shook it, and Bix looked over.

"Not a lot of water left, huh?" he said. It wasn't a question.

This was maybe enough water to cook dinner tonight and make coffee in the morning, plus a little to sip throughout the day. We still had a handful of watered-down beers, which we cinched into a mesh sack and dragged in the river behind our canoe to keep cool. (Coors Banquet is not an appropriate substitute for sufficient water, but this was our honeymoon, after all.) I wasn't *worried*, per se, but I wasn't exactly thrilled with the remaining volume of water.

If you've never seen the Green River, you might be wondering why water was a concern: Thousands of cubic feet of it flow past any given point on the river every second. But the Green River contains much more than just water. It's silty, so much so that most water filters are clogged almost immediately. It's also, according to the National Park Service, typically high in phosphorus, which can come from "fertilizers, detergents, human, domestic animal, and wild-life wastes, wind-deposited dust, soil leaching, and other geologic sources." This alone is enough to discourage me from drinking even filtered or treated water from the Green River. It also doesn't help that this area has a long history of mining for heavy metals; we would float past the now-defunct Hey Joe Uranium Mine later that day.

We were about to experience that paradox of the desert, its delicate balance between not enough and too much water. We pulled up at the mouth of Hell Roaring Canyon, slightly parched but not much worse for wear, after an abbreviated day of paddling. Our take-out point at Mineral Bottom was a little less than three miles downriver, and we were glad for the diminished output, considering our shrinking water supply.

We hiked a few hundred yards up Hell Roaring to the inscription of French fur trapper Denis Julien, which he'd carved into the rock wall in 1836. From our vantage point, we could see the canyon rim on the opposite side of the river, where ominous thunderheads had begun to gather.

"Is our camp okay at the mouth of this canyon?" I wondered aloud. The desert is notorious for flash flooding. A desert storm can mean a lot of rain all at once, and the soil contains lots of clay—it's not very absorbent, so it quickly becomes saturated, and the runoff gains steam. When it's all funneled into a low-lying area like a side canyon, this can add up to catastrophic damage.

We hurried back to the river and arrived just as the first fat drops of rain began to fall. The rapidly cooling temperature was a relief, but I was uneasy about our station so close to the mouth of a canyon. We briefly discussed loading the boat back up to float a bit farther downstream but dismissed the idea as lightning flashed on the canyon rim. This was not a good time to be on the water.

Instead, we moved the canoe a bit higher out of the river in case the water level rose. We quickly organized our gear so it would be ready to grab and load if we needed to leave in a hurry, then dove into the tent to ride out the storm.

And what a storm it was. The wind raged, bending our tent poles nearly horizontally. At one point, it was so loud—from thunder or rain and hail hitting the fly, I wasn't sure—I couldn't hear Bix talking to me from a few inches away.

I covered flash flooding in some detail in chapter 5. Our experience on Hawaii's Big Island wasn't all that unusual, which somehow feels right given that it's an equatorial island.

But it's not as uncommon as you might think in the arid desert. In their comprehensive *Over the Edge: Death in Grand Canyon,* which covers every known fatality in the park, Michael Ghiglieri and Thomas Myers count 14 flash flood fatalities in eight separate incidents between 1910 and 2012. That's a little less than a fatal flood every dozen years in Grand Canyon National Park, which is so enormous as to be truly awe-inspiring, but also makes up just a tiny percentage of the planet's desert landscapes.

That September was the end of what had proven to be an erratic monsoon season. In fact, on the very night we were worriedly watching the skies, there was a violent flash flood a little less than 200 miles south and west of us, as the raven flies, in the little town of Hildale, Utah. A massive thunderstorm—very likely part of the same system that blew over the Green River that night—dumped its contents near Hildale, and within minutes, Short Creek was transformed "from a trickle into a lethal torrent." The flood was forceful enough to wash away a vehicle, killing 13 people.

In nearby Zion National Park, 15 miles north of Hildale, seven people were killed in Keyhole Canyon in a flash flood resulting from the same storm. All seven were experienced hikers. None had canyoneering experience beyond a recent instructional class—not a red flag, since Keyhole is widely considered a fine slot canyon for first-timers.

Early on the morning of the group's hike, the Salt Lake City office of the National Weather Service forecast a 40 percent chance of rain for Zion National Park, specifically noting that there was a risk of flash flooding in slot canyons. The chance of rain was later bumped to 50 percent, and the *Los Angeles Times* reported that a ranger at the visitor center in Zion

> wrote on a cardboard sign near the wilderness desk that flash flooding that day was "probable." Rangers also informed people verbally when they sought permits. At least one other group also planned to visit the canyon.

Reports indicate that the group members were quite careful. The daughter of one of the couples killed said that her mother had the weather report written out and sitting in her camper, and another man had left the NOAA weather report pulled up on the cell phone later found in his truck.

It's impossible to say what the group thought—or thought they knew—that persuaded them to go into the slot canyon despite the flash flooding danger. I've more than once found myself thinking with an uncharacteristically sunny, glass-half-full mentality when an adventure I really want is on the line: *If it's a 40 percent chance of rain, that means there's a 60 percent chance it* won't *rain!* In a group that large, it's also easy to be lulled into assuming the danger must not be so bad if none of your six companions has spoken up. Either approach is fine if you're taking the dog for a walk around the block, less so if you're going for a hike above tree line, and, unfortunately, potentially fatal if you're venturing into a slot canyon.

Having been caught in many a surprise rainstorm with consequences ranging from "I wish I'd packed my rain jacket closer to the top of my backpack" to "I might need a rescue," I'm comfortable telling you I've made the mistakes I just mentioned. But, again, I'm not speculating as to whether that's what happened here—we'll never know, and it would be a disservice to these avid hikers' legacies to make assumptions about their thinking on the day of their accident. With that in mind, I urge you to consider the potential consequences of a flash flood and know that they are much more dire in the desert, particularly in a slot canyon or wash.

Flash flooding happens very suddenly, hence its name, which is why your best bet to survive a flash flood is to avoid being caught in one at all. (Remember this theme?) If there is rain in the forecast or if it has rained recently, steer clear of narrow constrictions, slot canyons, and washes. If you absolutely must travel in one of these places, keep your wits about you—watch the sky, listen carefully for the roar of incoming water, unbuckle your pack straps to give you a better chance of escaping your pack, should you be picked up by a flood—and have an exit strategy.

I'm sure my parents—and the shuttle driver we'd hired to pick us up at the end of our honeymoon—were worried, considering the news reports, but back on the banks of the Green, I had no idea that deadly Utah storms had killed 20 people that afternoon.

Fortunately, our habit of staking out the tent and rain fly tightly was deeply ingrained, and when the maelstrom abated half an hour later, we'd stayed dry. I unzipped the door and poked my head out, half-expecting to be met with a wall of muddy water as it roared down the canyon, but luck had been on our side. We moved our camp a bit farther from the mouth of the canyon, in case another storm rolled through or a delayed flash flood gathered steam. I was a little nervous, but the only consequence of our camping too close to a wash was a restless night.

The next morning, we broke camp early and made a speedy run to Mineral Bottom. Moments later, the shuttle we'd hired pulled up. The driver spotted us and shuffled over to help us load our already-dry gear into his red Bronco.

"I thought you guys might be down here another day or two," he laughed. The 16-mile road to Mineral Bottom is notorious for its tight, steep switchbacks, which become impassable when they're wet.

"Us too," I chuckled. The storm had been nerve-wracking, but also extraordinarily beautiful, a reminder of just how powerful this place was. We would have been very thirsty if we'd had to wait an extra day for our shuttle—plus, I was practically euphoric at the thought of one last chocolate malt at Milt's Stop & Eat, now just an hour away, before we left Moab—but there are worse places to extend one's honeymoon.

Cedar Mesa occupies some 400 square miles of southeastern Utah. It's hemmed in by some of the area's most iconic geographical features: Comb Wash and Grand Gulch in the east and west, respectively; Elk Ridge to the north; and the gorge carved by the San Juan River to the south. Characteristically for the American Southwest, the climate is due in part to its high elevation: Most of Cedar Mesa sits over 4,000 feet above sea level, and it reaches altitudes of 6,500 feet.

This high plateau is emblematic of the desert landscape in this part of the planet. It's also brimming with human history. Clovis people hunted and lived on Cedar Mesa as long as 13,000 years ago, and today, the area is home to countless archaeological artifacts, including ancient dwellings, from Ancestral Puebloans.

That's part of the reason most of Cedar Mesa was included in Bears Ears National Monument, which then-president Barack Obama established via the Antiquities Act in December 2016. A year later, Obama's successor slashed the 1.3-million-acre monument by 85 percent in order to appease energy companies who wanted to mine fossil fuels and uranium deposits. There's a constant push and pull between environmentalists and recreators who don't want to see pristine wilderness destroyed and the need for energy companies to keep up with growing demand. I do understand the need for the latter. I drive a car that requires fossil fuels to operate, and though I work to reduce my carbon footprint, I'm a consumer and thus part of the reason fossil fuels are in high demand.

But Bears Ears and its environs are more than pristine wilderness or wildlife habitat important to the greater ecosystem of the Southwest, though all those things are true. Bears Ears—what *should* be Bears Ears—is filled with more than 100,000 cultural artifacts that shape the story of human existence. The landscape is extremely important to the Navajo Nation, Ute Mountain Ute Tribe, and Hopi Nation. What you'll find at Cedar Mesa is irreplaceable.

The fight for Bears Ears rages on as of this writing. It's obvious where I stand on the matter, and like so many other visitors to this hallowed place, I can make my most convincing argument with a story of my own interactions with it. The caveat: In order to really understand what's so special about Bears Ears, you'll have to visit yourself.

One Memorial Day weekend, our friends Hale and Angela flew from Seattle to Grand Junction, where Bix and I picked them up and drove to Moab. We spent a couple of nights camped in Castle Valley, hiked at Dead Horse Point State Park, and took the popular trail to Corona Arch. In late May, it was already hot enough that the poor, normally peppy Bodhi lay down under the shade of a pinyon pine on our first hike, prompting Angela and me to wait with him in the shade while Hale and Bix went to fetch the car. (I felt like the worst dog owner on the planet and resolved to start subsequent hikes earlier in the morning.)

As Moab filled up for the holiday weekend, we headed south toward Cedar Mesa, where we hoped to escape the crowds. We planned an overnight backpacking trip in Road Canyon, a 12-mile out-and-back route that we figured would be a relatively easy outing, especially if we split the hike over two days.*

Road Canyon is a "credit card hike," a term often ascribed to hikes that begin with a downhill. When you climb a mountain, you get the bigger effort—the uphill hike—out of the way first. If you can hike up the mountain, all things being equal, you can probably get back down it. With canyon hiking, on the other hand, you take out some "credit" on the first half of the hike into the canyon, which is entirely downhill. Then you have to pay it back on the way out, when you're hiking uphill.

At the far end of Road Canyon, miles from the dusty, poorly marked trailhead where we'd left our truck, is a site called Seven

---

* We picked this hike in part because it's known for the ruins you can spot from the trail, and because it's one of a few canyon hikes on Cedar Mesa where dogs are allowed. This is crucial to maintaining the sites' archaeological integrity: If you're bringing a dog, be sure you're avoiding areas where they're specifically prohibited. Dogs, even ones as well behaved as Bodhi, absolutely must remain on-leash the entire time. Bix and I took turns holding our dog's leash from the trail and hiking up to check out the granaries and kivas up close.

Kivas—this is why it was worth it to us to take out the credit. We planned to follow the canyon to the archaeological site. If we found a campsite on the way, great; we'd drop our heavy packs there and set up camp, then continue to Seven Kivas carrying only some water and snacks. If not, we'd carry our packs the whole way, then look harder for a site on the way back.

The night before our hike brought a blinding windstorm, and we woke up with tents (and eyes and nostrils and throats) full of dust. Still, the morning started off almost magically: It was pleasantly cool, with temperatures in the mid-70s, and the rising sun bounced playfully off the scrappy juniper and towering sandstone cliffs. As we scrambled deeper into the canyon, we started to spot evidence of its ancient residents high overhead.

We stopped a few times to squint at granaries tucked into protected bands of cliff, and my head spun at the thought that people regularly managed to get in and out of these seemingly inaccessible storage spots.

As the morning wore on, we started looking harder for campsites. There wasn't much: There are few flat spots in Road Canyon, and the rare flat patch of ground is often covered in cactus (ouch) or cryptobiotic soil, which can take centuries to recover from a single footprint, let alone a tent.

At one point, we dropped packs to scout a spot that seemed like it might work. The four of us split up—we'd all identified plenty of backcountry campsites before, so we agreed to meet back at our pile of backpacks in 10 or 15 minutes. I scrambled up to a promising-looking ledge with a sweeping view of the canyon, and just as I was about to mark the spot in my GPS app, I felt the hair on the back of my neck stand up.

I wheeled around to see a little kettle—a depression in the soft sandstone where a pool of rainwater had collected—and the unmistakable, still-wet pawprints of a large feline leading away from it, into the bushes. With so few reasonable spots to sleep in Road Canyon, it appeared this one was already occupied.

I bumped into Angela as I hurried back to the group. Alarmed by the close encounter, we scurried across the narrow sandstone ledge leading to our packs, where we told Hale and Bix about the erstwhile campsite. I was very glad to be in a group of four humans and a dog, which even a bold mountain lion would likely prefer to avoid.

From the lion's lair, we continued down the canyon, first employing a bit of creative route-finding that led us to a granary vantage point with no obvious way down, then backtracking and traversing a sandstone gulch that funneled into a bottomless-looking pool of stagnant water. Both were made more difficult by our heavy overnight packs, which I would later wish we'd just stashed farther up-canyon.

At this point, I was glad for our extensive combined route-finding experience. We did have a GPS, a topo map and compass, and a description of the hike, but none was detailed enough to show us all the potential missteps. If a topo map has 100-foot contours, for example, you can still find yourself staring at a 90-foot cliff: It's not big enough to appear on your map, but it's certainly big enough to present a problem. Road Canyon was challenging even with our combined years of finding off-trail routes in the backcountry.

Five hours after we left the trailhead, we arrived at an enormous overhang. The air felt 10 degrees cooler in the shade. We dropped our packs and scanned above for the Seven Kivas.

We picked out the site by searching for the midden, a pile of ancient rubble that functioned as the discard heap for the kivas. A few at a time, we scrambled up a makeshift midden trail to the kivas.

Staring into these centuries-old rooms, some of which still contained mummified corn cobs, felt more intimate than I'd expected. I could pick out fingerprints in the plaster walls: The people who built these kivas had *fingerprints*. Of course they did, and yet there was something so stirring about this revelation—an individual human, not some hypothetical being, had built this sturdy structure, and I was standing in their presence hundreds of years later. If I can be overcome by a feeling—one I can describe only as awe—this powerful with minimal knowledge of the people who came before me, I can't imagine what the descendants of those Ancestral Puebloans must feel at Seven Kivas, or at any of the thousands of other sites at Cedar Mesa.

Once we'd all been sufficiently amazed, our group circled up back at the base of the midden, where I rummaged through my pack and pulled out a few not-quite-cold beverages to share. We sat in silence in the shade for a few minutes, thinking about what we'd just experienced (except Bodhi, whose entire trip was centered around hatching Wile E. Coyote-style plots to catch lizards).

Bix finally broke the silence. "I think we have to accept the possibility that this is a day hike," he mused.

I groaned. He was right, of course—this was an out-and-back hike, which meant we'd already passed any potential campsite on the hike to Seven Kivas. It seemed unlikely that we'd missed anything.

There was, in fact, no appropriate campsite in Road Canyon for a group of four people with two tents, at least not one that we could find. When we finally arrived back at our truck at the Road Canyon trailhead, nearly 1,000 vertical feet above Seven Kivas, we were bone tired—even Bodhi, who'd finally succeeded in pouncing on and catching a small lizard despite being on a leash. (When Bix instructed him to "Drop it!" Bodhi opened his mouth, and the little creature popped out and scuttled away, apparently unharmed.)

Fortunately, we'd brought plenty of water, assuming our trip would be an overnight one. It was a little cooler down in the canyon than it was north of us in Moab, and we'd maximized our time in the pleasant temperatures by starting our hike before it was fully light outside.

A predawn start is often associated with climbing at altitude, but it's crucial for desert hiking, too, when midday temperatures can soar well into the triple digits. Years later, my family—my parents, who were celebrating their 35th wedding anniversary, Bix, and I—signed on for a guided river trip through the Grand Canyon. It began at the traditional put-in at Lees Ferry, and our expedition terminated six days later and 87 river miles downstream at Phantom Ranch, where we were replaced by a fresh cadre of passengers.

We arrived in early August, a month whose record high at Phantom Ranch is 120 degrees. That's exceedingly hot, but average temperatures regularly soar above 100 degrees. Our group spent an evening exploring Phantom Ranch, then set our alarms for the actual crack of dawn in order to take advantage of the darkness and accompanying coolness on our hike to the South Rim via the Bright Angel Trail.

As I write this from my home in Boise, we're in the middle of a heat wave: Temperatures will be near or even exceed 100 degrees every day for the next week. That's hot enough for the National Weather Service to issue an excessive heat warning for southwestern Idaho. The agency recommends drinking plenty of fluids, staying out of the sun, and checking up on relatives and neighbors. These are the suggested precautions for going about day-to-day tasks like working in the yard or driving to and from work, so by this standard, a strenuous activity like hiking nearly 9.5 miles and 4,400 vertical feet from Phantom Ranch to the South Rim would be entirely out of the question. But every year, at least a handful of people assume it'll be cooler below the rim and attempt a hike from the South Rim in triple-digit temperatures.

Bright Angel Trail, as hiked from the South Rim, is the ultimate credit card hike. If you start from the rim nice and early, you take advantage of the cooler temps, and the downhill travel is deceptive—by the numbers, it would be easy to think you're halfway done with the hike when you've made it to the Colorado River. But the effort required to pay back the next 9.5 miles and 4,380 feet of elevation between you and the rim is going to cost a lot more than what you've spent getting down here.

The problem is that once you make it to Phantom Ranch, the only way to get back to the South Rim is with a long, hot hike that gains a great deal of elevation. There's no easy way to organize a rescue from the bottom of the Grand Canyon. If you've made the trek down to the river and find yourself spent, your best bet is to wait until evening, when the heat of the day has passed. The National Park Service specifically warns hikers not to attempt to hike from the South Rim to Phantom Ranch and back in a single day, especially between May and September. Ghiglieri and Myers count 52 victims of heat stroke between 1894 and 2012, plus another 39 deaths by heat-induced cardiac arrest. On the Bright Angel Trail specifically, more than a dozen people have died of heat stroke or heat-induced cardiac arrest while attempting to hike from the rim to some point below and back again on the same day.

Even people with a great deal of experience at keeping themselves hydrated can succumb to the extreme environment of the desert. In 2004, distance runner Margaret Bradley ran the Boston Marathon in just over three hours. That year's race was particularly hot—85 degrees in humid Boston—and more than a thousand runners had to be treated for dehydration. Not Bradley, who would tell the *Chicago Athlete* (she was a med student at the University of Chicago) that she'd managed to perform so admirably at the race because she'd focused on staying hydrated.

That July, Bradley and a companion set out for an ambitious Grand Canyon run. The pair departed from the Grandview Trail at 8:00 a.m., long after sunrise, and headed down the Tonto Trail. (The National Park Service classifies this trail as "not recommended during summer" due to its lack of shade.) Their intended route was nearly 30 miles. Neither carried sufficient water for the outing.

That afternoon, write Ghiglieri and Myers, the pair separated. As the mercury soared above 100 degrees, Bradley's companion finished his water and began to feel exhausted.

> Bradley, now worried not just about their combined plight but about [her companion's] deteriorating condition, would continue onward alone, even though she too was out of water and even more dehydrated than [him].

Bradley's companion understood that she intended to run to Phantom Ranch and arrange a rescue for him. A few hours after they separated, he roused himself from his dehydrated stupor and pressed on, eventually running into a US Geological Survey employee who hiked him back to the rim and drove him back to Flagstaff. The companion also encountered a hiking guide headed for Phantom Ranch, and asked them to tell Bradley when they arrived that he was alright and hiking out of the canyon. He never did report her missing; 38 hours would pass between their separation and Bradley's being listed as a missing person, which occurred because she didn't show up to meet her family in Flagstaff. The next day, SAR crews found her curled in fetal position in a terrain trap, where she had died of dehydration.

Humans need water to survive. We're mostly made of it; our very blood is 90 percent water. The hotter the environment we're in, the more fluid we need to function properly. When we're exercising strenuously, especially in the heat, we lose water by sweating, breathing, and metabolizing. Dehydration contributes to fatigue, often causing people to make mistakes they wouldn't otherwise. Feeling tired and irritable are often early signs. You should also be vigilant of output—that is, urine. "A happy mountaineer always pees clear," goes the old adage, and it applies to hikers in the desert, too. Dark, smelly urine is an indication that your body is low on water. As dehydration progresses, it can result in headaches, dizziness, and an altered mental state. In extreme cases, the body might exhibit signs typical of shock, like a rapid heartbeat, nausea, and pale, clammy skin.

Dehydration can also be cumulative, meaning a negative water balance can build up over days, and it manifests with many of the same symptoms as hypothermia, altitude sickness, heat stroke, and fatigue. Because it's often closely intertwined with those ailments, the key is knowing to look for signs of dehydration early. Better yet, prevent it altogether by carrying and drinking plenty of fluids on a hot day.*

The Walker family had arrived at Phantom Ranch by the most fun means possible: via the Colorado River. In other words, we didn't start the upward journey halfway through our hike, but at the very beginning. We were freshly showered, well fed, and generally bright-eyed and bushy-tailed in the wee hours of that morning. Now our biggest challenge would be to stay hydrated throughout our hike. This is relatively easy to do on the Bright Angel Trail, which has four rest stops with drinking water along the way,† meaning you don't have to lug all the heavy water you'll need for a hike this long.

By the time we emerged from the canyon on the crowded South Rim, an ice-cold Coke had never sounded so good. Bix and I sat in the shade for a few minutes, then wandered over to the

---

* It is possible to drink too much water, resulting in a condition called hyponatremia, or water intoxication. It's understandable: We're told to take on plenty of fluids in hot climates, so it can be tempting to chug too much too quickly. The symptoms are strikingly similar to those of dehydration: nausea, headache, possibly bloating. If you're experiencing those symptoms and have recently consumed lots of water (say, a few liters in the last couple of hours), hyponatremia is the more likely culprit than dehydration, and it's best to stop drinking and get out of the sun. If things don't improve quickly thereafter, seek medical attention.
† Water is available seasonally at three of these rest houses and year-round at Indian Gardens. In any case, check with the National Park Service before you begin your hike to make sure you understand where water will be available before you start hiking.

nearest cafeteria for cold drinks. As we shuffled back to the top of the trail to wait for my parents to arrive, I felt a wave of gratitude that we'd all be done hiking soon. The heat felt oppressively heavy.

"God, it's hot," I panted to Bix, taking a breathless swig of my soda.

"Yeah," he agreed. "But at least it's a dry heat."

LESSONS LEARNED

- **Carry more water than you think you need.** I can't think of a situation that wouldn't be made worse by dehydration. In many regions, where you might have the opportunity to fill up and purify water at streams and lakes, you can get away with carrying just a liter or two of water at a time. But bodies of water in the desert are fickle, and you shouldn't count on one to save your bacon. Where they are found, they're often too silty to filter sufficiently for drinking water—take the Green and Colorado Rivers, for example. The National Park Service recommends drinking a gallon of water per day in the Grand Canyon during the warm months. That doesn't include the water you'll need for cooking or handwashing if you're on an extended trip. A gallon of water weighs around eight pounds. If the total weight of the water you'd need to carry to meet the gallon-a-day threshold is prohibitively heavy, you're better off planning a shorter trip or rescheduling for a time when you've trained to carry more weight.

- **Protect yourself from the sun.** Humans have developed lots of ways to protect ourselves from the run, ranging from high-quality sunscreen to the full skin coverage I opted for on my honeymoon. The best way to protect your body from the full bore of the sun, though, is to avoid hiking during the hottest parts of the day. In many desert regions, that's between 10:00 a.m. and 4:00 p.m., when the sun is highest in the sky and shade is scarcest. Plan your hikes to be done before solar noon, then take a break and hydrate when things are hottest.

- **Watch the weather.** In many regions, knowing the forecast just for the day you plan to travel is sufficient to keep you safe. Not so in the desert. Flash floods can take many hours to gather upstream, so a heavy storm the day before your outing can render your intended route extremely dangerous. When possible, consult the local land manager—whether it's the National Park Service, the US Forest Service, or the Bureau of Land Management—about conditions where you plan to hike, especially during monsoon season. On the other side of the coin, it's worth knowing whether the day of your planned outing is going to be exceptionally hot. In that case, hiking during the cooler morning and evening is doubly important, and you'll want to be armed with even more water (and possibly an electrolyte supplement).

- **Hone your navigational skills.** Route-finding relies on obvious markers—handrails—that help you contextualize your location. In the desert, particularly in canyon country, the scale can be difficult to comprehend, and handrails can be tough to spot from a given vantage point. If you're hiking a route for the first time, use extra caution. If I'm traveling somewhere I've never been before, I download a map to the GPS app on my phone *and* bring a paper map and compass (I want a backup in case my phone overheats). If you choose to scramble up something for a better look or as a means to get where you're going, pause to check in with yourself regularly to make sure you can climb back down.

CHAPTER TEN

Blackstone Bay, Revisited

I MOVED TO ALASKA WHEN I WAS 22. I'M STILL NOT SURE IF I WAS searching for something or looking to get away from something, and in that way, I'm very much a stereotype: untethered youth who figures they'll find answers on the Last Frontier.

The best known example of this phenomenon is, of course, Christopher McCandless—the subject of Jon Krakauer's piece in *Outside* magazine, which was subsequently turned into a book and, eventually, a blockbuster film—who started his journey north to Alaska in 1990. He was scarcely older than I was when my own odyssey began.

By the time he wound up in Fairbanks in 1992, at age 24, McCandless (known to many of the friends he made during his travels as Alexander Supertramp) had been on the road for nearly two years. He abandoned his beloved car, donated his life savings to Oxfam, and hitchhiked from one town to the next, working only as long as he needed to in order to save up enough to keep moving.

You probably already know how this story ends. McCandless hiked into the Alaskan backcountry, which the writer Chip Brown described in the *New Yorker* in 1993 as "the Alaska that belongs as much to the estate of the imagination as to the actual earth," with minimal supplies. He forded the Teklanika River, which, in April, was not yet the raging torrent he would encounter months later.

He found an abandoned bus, occasionally used as a winter hunting base camp, where he set up shop.

There, his life was the simple existence he'd dreamed about. He read a tattered copy of *Doctor Zhivago*. He shot small game and eventually a moose, whose carcass he didn't know how to process correctly. He was idealistic and unprepared, but then so are a lot of kids who head up to Alaska, myself included.

Eventually, McCandless starved to death, perhaps because of a poisonous plant he'd misidentified and consumed. By then, in his malnourished state, he would not have been able to recross the Teklanika, now swollen with glacial runoff and snowmelt. He likely died late that summer, and hunters discovered his body in the fall of 1992.

In the decades since his death, McCandless has become something of a focal point in the adventure community. Some see him as a folk hero, a young man who couldn't live in the modern world. Others, including many Alaskans, point to him as yet another example of the ignorant outsider: He approached the Alaskan backcountry without sufficient respect for the magnitude of life in the bush and, unsurprisingly, paid the ultimate price.

One such Alaskan detractor is Craig Medred, a prominent Anchorage reporter known for his coverage of Alaskan accidents and his scathing commentary on those who make backcountry mistakes. In an op-ed on McCandless, he refers to the young man as a "bum, poacher, and thief."

Medred's writing on various misfortunes in the wilds of Alaska is widely known among longtime locals. My friend Joe Stock, a well-known guide and avalanche educator, once taped a picture of Medred to his skis. He looks at it when he's considering making a risky decision and wonders: *What would Craig Medred write about me if I died doing this?* (It works: Stock is one of the best and most conservative guides I know.)

When I crossed the border from the Yukon territory in 2012, I had not yet heard of Craig Medred or Joe Stock, but I definitely knew who Chris McCandless was. My then-boyfriend and I drove his Toyota 4Runner from Colorado, where I'd just finished my undergraduate degree and decided that a life as a high school teacher wasn't for me. I'd gotten into a graduate program at Alaska Pacific University (APU), and he agreed to come with me, despite that we'd never lived together before.

Immediately after we arrived and signed a lease on an apartment in Wasilla, I embarked on my very first Alaskan adventure: a weeklong sea kayaking trip in Prince William Sound, a program the university set up for incoming freshmen and other new students. I left my boyfriend at home to unpack all our worldly possessions.

Years later, my memories of the trip are hazy. I felt much older than the squirrelly 17- and 18-year-old freshmen, but that didn't really bother me. I wasn't there to meet people; I was there to see wild Alaska. Our group set out from Whittier with a smattering of single and double kayaks, meaning that students alternated between having a partner and paddling alone.

We reached Squirrel Cove, about eight miles from Whittier, on our first day of paddling. The rain started not long after we set up camp on the wooden tent platforms, and it continued in earnest into the next morning.

My tentmate and I woke up and padded down to the beach for coffee on the first backcountry morning of the trip. Our trip leader, the university's academic dean, was already there. The marine radio was on, and a robotic voice advised us that we could expect "seas five feet," meaning that we'd encounter five-foot waves in much of the Western Sound. We stayed put.

Rain continued into the following day, but by then, the seas had apparently abated. Perhaps because I was older or because I had some backcountry experience (or maybe thanks to luck of the draw), I was in a single kayak that day.

We crossed the yawning mouth of Blackstone Bay in fog thick enough that I could barely make out the land on the other side. The seas were probably only two or three feet, but they felt enormous to me. Anytime I didn't have the nose of my boat perpendicular to the waves, I felt awfully precarious. By the time we reached camp that afternoon, I was on the verge of tears.

I'm basically Chris McCandless, I remember thinking, though obviously the trip leaders had no intention of leaving me alone or allowing me to starve to death.

Fortunately, my self-pity didn't last long. We awoke the next morning to clear blue skies. We paddled from our campsite to 17 Mile Beach, so named for its distance from Whittier, where we laid out our sopping gear. The following morning, we awoke to icebergs on the beach—they'd been left behind by the receding tide. We paddled as close as protocol allowed to the glaciers, then fell asleep to the sounds of them calving into the bay.

On the last day of our trip, the weather moved back in and a water taxi picked us up and brought us back to Whittier. It was, I would later learn, all quintessential Alaska—the fast-moving weather, the short window of perfect conditions. I was hooked.

My boyfriend was very glad to see me when I arrived home unscathed. Though he was an avid hiker himself, I imagine these extended backcountry forays worried him, and my thoughtless 22-year-old self didn't think twice about leaving him in the lurch when the opportunity to go out for a week (or two or three or a month, as I'd do later) arose. Six months later, when I returned home early from a backcountry trip due to a couple of frostbitten toes and spent the next week explaining why I'd need to be gone the next several weekends to ice climb, I had pushed him to his breaking point.

As you've probably surmised, things didn't work out between us. Of course, every relationship is different, but when you boil it down, I simply didn't make the time for a boyfriend—to say nothing of the time a significant other needs when they've moved 4,000 miles to be with you and don't know another soul in the area.

When my very nice now-ex moved from Alaska to Montana, I felt guilty, but I couldn't articulate why. I didn't regret having gone on the Blackstone Bay trip—who in their right mind, I figured, would have turned down a chance like that? But nobody wants to be the one stuck at home unpacking, starting a new chapter in life alone. It wasn't malicious, but it was certainly thoughtless, and anyway it doesn't matter because the result is the same: I hurt someone I cared about, and then I kept doing it. If I'd known then how important it would become to me to be gone, I'd have told him sooner. It's a mistake I would take to heart.

It would be the better part of a decade—not to mention a graduate degree and a marriage—before I'd return to Blackstone Bay, this time with my significant other in tow. In the intervening years, I was focused on finishing my degree and skiing whenever possible. I went on a handful of sea kayaking trips, but it would take time for me to decide that something other than standing on a summit was a worthy use of my time and limited funds.

Four years after I'd left Alaska for Colorado, I returned with my husband and two friends for a trip in Blackstone Bay. We rented two double boats—I wasn't about to re-create my scary crossing in a single kayak—and arranged to have a water taxi drop us off at 13 Mile, near the beach where my group had spent a rainy night seven years earlier. From there, we planned to paddle to Willard Island, which sits squarely in the middle of the bay, and set up a base camp for a couple of days of touring the bay. On the fourth and final day of our trip, we'd paddle back to Whittier.

To prepare for my return to Blackstone Bay, I emailed Paul Twardock, who was the chair of the Outdoor Studies department when I attended APU. He'd written a guidebook to sea kayaking in Prince William Sound, and, having resolved to do considerably more research now that I didn't have a trip leader to save my bacon, I wanted a copy to know what I was up against.

"Emma," Paul wrote in the copy he sent me, "Happy and safe paddling!"

I didn't know how complex it could be to paddle safely in Prince William Sound.

The first two days of our trip were relatively uneventful. I'd brought along a detailed paper map and compass and downloaded a nautical chart to my phone, which doubled as a GPS device. We were also armed with a two-way radio, though it didn't work within the confines of Blackstone Bay—I'd assumed it would.

Also on this trip were two of our closest friends, Hale and Angela, who'd taken an in-depth sea kayaking class through the Mountaineers, a Seattle-based outdoor club. I was confident in setting up camp, calling "Hey, bear!" whenever we were on land, and cooking on the rock beach. Still, on the water, I depended on their expertise to navigate, understand the tides, and, though I sincerely hoped it wouldn't come to this, organize a rescue if necessary.

It only took us an hour and a half of paddling and one quiet crossing in near-perfect conditions to find our campsite at Willard Island. We saw a handful of sea otters along the way, and I struggled to pull my camera out in time to capture them before they disappeared beneath the surface, which they can do for up to five minutes at a time.

I'd later learn that sea otters, though they appear cute and cuddly, can actually be quite aggressive. The vast majority of sea otters live in coastal Alaska, where they can produce pups any time of year. Unlike their riparian counterparts, sea otters can weigh up to 90 pounds—like a big, cranky Labrador retriever. Scientifically speaking, they're part of the family that includes such carnivorous creatures as the badger, skunk, weasel, and wolverine, so they're not messing around. Their bite is powerful enough to break human bones, and I imagine they thought I owed them a bit more respect as I cooed over them on this trip.

The campsite where we erected our tents had clearly been used before and was well out of the tidal zone; large trees, including one where a bald eagle had set up its nest, surrounded our tent site. We spent that first afternoon drinking lukewarm beer, lounging in the prolonged sunlight of the Alaskan summer, and taking in the glaciers all around us.

The following day, we battled strong headwinds as we paddled to the terminus of Willard Island to see the enormous calving glaciers. When we reached the very tip of the island, I scouted for an easy point to cross back to the mainland and paddle close to the shore, given the two-foot seas and that the tide was working against us.

Almost as soon as we left the sheltered shoreline of Willard Island, Bix and I began to feel the tide pulling us to the north, where the waves looked considerably bigger. It was as if someone had taken a gigantic ruler and drawn a straight line between Willard and the protected coastline along Blackstone Bay. On one side of the line were gentle waves; on the other were whitecaps.

This line, as it turns out, was not a figment of my imagination. In summer 1989, a group of six kayakers—three of whom had no previous sea kayaking experience—had a water taxi deposit them at 17 Mile, where I spent two nights on my first-ever foray into Blackstone Bay. They planned to tour for a couple of days and be picked up by a water taxi at Squirrel Cove, where I spent the first two nights of that trip (and where, seven years later, I'd spend the last night of my trip). Importantly, though they had topographical maps, the group did not carry a nautical chart.

The line I noticed on my latter trip is created by a submerged glacial moraine, which sits just 1.25 fathoms beneath the surface at mean low tide, while the ocean floor on either side of it is 25 fathoms deep. You don't have to be able to convert fathoms to feet to understand that this creates an underwater wall; the sudden steepness means waves, too, steepen and break. When water breaks over a sandbar or glacial moraine, there's a possibility of tide rips. These can easily flip a kayak, and larger boats can't hope to cross without running aground.

When the 1989 party didn't show up at Squirrel Cove at the appointed time, their water taxi hurried into Blackstone Bay in hopes of intercepting them, given the less-than-ideal conditions. But the charter boat couldn't cross the shallow moraine.

This meant another night out for the group of six. I can guess at what those kayakers were feeling—the disquieting knowledge that your ride and your loved ones are waiting for you to show up. It didn't help that the winds picked up, threatening to collapse their tents, and that—thinking they'd soon be back in Whittier—some of the group had packed hastily that morning, and their remaining clothes were too wet to keep them warm.

I've been snowed into my tent for days at a time, willing the clouds to disperse so I can see where I'm going. I know the sinking feeling of whittling away at my diminishing food supply and knowing that, if the weather keeps up for another couple of days, I'll be terribly hungry and have an even harder time making my way back to civilization. Still, a handful of hungry days is often distinctly preferable to making a go of it too soon, when conditions dictate staying put. It's a tough balance.

As I read the account of this incident in Twardock's book, my heart ached for the kayakers trapped in Blackstone Bay, which I'd always thought of as a verdant paradise. When the conditions didn't improve, their supplies dwindled until they felt they had no choice but to make a desperate gambit for the mainland and hug the shoreline until they reached Squirrel Cove.

"The fourth day the group tried again to paddle north into strong winds and waves," Twardock explains.

As they encountered the tidal rip caused by the submerged moraine east of VABM [vertical angle benchmark] Inner, the boats started to turn sideways to the wind and waves. The waves suddenly became very steep (up to five feet), and three of the four boats flipped.

A tide rip is just as scary as it sounds, and to make matters more confusing, it's not the same thing as a riptide. A riptide is an offshore current that's strongest where flows are constricted. They mostly occur in the ocean, but if an inland body of water is big enough—say, the Great Lakes—they're a possibility. (Bix remembers swimming at the beach near his childhood home as a little boy and feeling the unshakable pull of a Lake Michigan riptide grabbing at his ankles.)

A tide rip, on the other hand, is a turbulent stretch of water caused by one current flowing across another—exactly the sort of thing that might happen when a glacial moraine builds up just below the surface, causing the tides to seemingly flow in opposite directions. These opposing forces often occur at a shallow point like the one off the tip of Willard Island, and they have no trouble flipping a small boat like a sea kayak.

The boat that stayed upright could not help the others, but managed to get to Willard Island. One person was able to get on top of her boat, but not re-enter it, and kick herself to Willard Island. The other single kayaker also made it to Willard by alternately swimming and curling up in a fetal position to stay warm. The two men in the second double died, most likely of hypothermia.

Hypothermia wasn't just a possibility because it was raining on the day of this accident. The danger of hypothermia is close at hand anytime you're paddling, even on a warm summer day, especially in

Alaska. Water—particularly water that's filled with icebergs and is thus much colder than the seawater you might encounter on a warm beach outside Alaska—has a way of cooling the human body, particularly when it's paired with wind.

The principles of convection and conduction exacerbate the feeling of cold when the body is wet. When you're surrounded by something cold, like air or water, the speed at which it makes *you* cold depends on how much colder it is than your body temperature, how much of your body is exposed to it, and how well insulated you are. The average water temperature in Prince William Sound fluctuates according to the season, but in the season most people paddle, it's rarely warmer than 56 degrees Fahrenheit, and often 10 degrees colder. In other words, if your entire body is suddenly thrust underwater—and you're rarely paddling in insulated gear, most of which does little when it's wet—you're likely to become very cold very quickly.

The principle of convection is similar—it's the process of heat leaving your body when you're in direct contact with cold air or water. Again, when you're almost fully submerged, heat can escape quickly, and hypothermia sets in fast.

When you're thrown into cold water with or without warning, there's a moment where everything pauses. No matter what you think you're prepared for, it's almost impossible to gasp for breath; the sudden cold is a shock to the system. It's challenging enough to keep your head above the surface, thus following your body's deeply held survival instinct to keep your airway clear, let alone flip a swamped kayak back over or clamber back into it. The folks from the 1989 group who managed to reboard their boats and kick their way back to shore were undoubtedly working with pure adrenaline.

The water in Blackstone Bay is chilly even at the height of summer. During my latter trip in late June (just days after the solstice, when the sun is still making some of its longest appearances in the sky), the water hovered at just over 50 degrees Fahrenheit.

It was littered with remnants of the surrounding glaciers—some icebergs were small enough to grab from the cockpit; others were larger than our double kayak and doubtless weighed far more—and a swim seemed almost unthinkable. Add the cooling power of the wind, and a swim would likely be terribly unpleasant. If you were too far from shore, it would be deadly.

Despite not having yet read Twardock's account of the 1989 party's tragedy—and having the advantage of relatively benign headwinds and quiet tides—we heeded the warning signs and tracked just south of the tide rip.

We stopped to fill up our water bladders at the rocky point between the Blackstone and Beloit Glaciers. Here, a healthy glacial stream flowed steadily out to sea; we pulled our boats onto the beach and tromped upstream in our rubber boots to a point where the water flowed freely. (Stagnant points allow bacteria to build up and create a breeding ground for diseases such as giardia, which can make a person terribly sick.)

After a quick break, we reboarded our double kayaks to paddle across the open water near the Beloit Glacier.

It's something special to paddle near a glacier that terminates into the sea. We'd spent the previous night listening to the glaciers calve into Prince William Sound, and one of my fondest memories of my first Alaskan expedition was falling asleep to the white noise of ice chunks heaving themselves into the water. It sounds very much like thunder.

Of course, a large chunk of ice falling into a body of water is liable to create an enormous tidal wave—the kind that can easily capsize small boats.

That happened in June 1993, when a couple of sea kayakers touring in the bay got too close to Blackstone Glacier. The glacier is named for a miner who, in 1896, attempted to carry a load of mail from Cook Inlet (the body of water on which Anchorage sits) to Whittier and disappeared in a snowstorm, never to be heard from again. His brother, Willard—after whom the island on which my friends and I camped was later named—followed him into the wilderness to search, only to find the seemingly untouched packet of mail and not another trace.

In 1993, after a day of touring the bay and watching the glacial activity, two kayakers in separate boats paddled up to the glacier to fill a water bottle with runoff. When chunks of ice detached from the glacier and fell into the water below, one of the kayakers was knocked unconscious. His companion, a nurse, grabbed onto his boat and paddled them both to the nearest beach, where she immobilized his broken arm and reset his dislocated shoulder.

The problem, then, was that she couldn't leave the injured man—who was vacillating in and out of consciousness—alone to get help, fearing he would die without her supervision. She attempted to tow him in his boat back to their camp, but the current from the incoming tide was too strong, and she had to pull off and wait for it to slow down. Finally, in the wee hours of the next morning, she managed to tow her injured partner into camp, where the rest of the group (including a physician's assistant) did their best to warm him up and stabilize him. Eventually, though, he lost consciousness altogether, and he never responded to the group's CPR efforts. An autopsy would later show that he died of the trauma he'd sustained to his head and chest.

I think about this scenario a lot. I'm less disturbed by the possibility that something might happen to me than the idea that my spouse or a friend might be struck by an objective hazard. If my boat capsized and Bix was rendered comatose by a falling chunk of ice, would I have the wherewithal to get him to shore, stabilize him, and get outside help in time to save his life? I can't help but think the rest of my nights would be beset with nightmares of his lifeless face, losing color as I paddled desperately for help. As morbid as this might sound, it forces me into clearheadedness as I jockey for a better photo of the calving glaciers—what photo could possibly be worth my life, let alone that of the person I love most?

This scenario sat heavy on my mind as we paddled past the Beloit, whose right side, on this warm day, was flanked by a violent rooster tail of a waterfall. No pieces of ice calved as we paddled past the glacier, but we kept the half-mile distance Twardock prescribes in his book.

As we rejoined the mainland on the other side of the little inlet, countless small icebergs came into view. I thought of the RMS *Titanic*, which sank in 1912 in the North Atlantic, taking more than 1,500 souls with it, when it struck an iceberg in the middle of the night. This comparison is a bit dramatic, but it's impossible not to notice that the relatively small icebergs whose tops poke above the surface of the water are considerably larger underwater, and that it wouldn't take much for one such piece of ice to smash my relatively fragile sea kayak to smithereens.

As we navigated between the icebergs, I happened to glance at the shore, where a platoon of kayaks had beached. We'd planned to land here and harvest a couple of the smaller bergs to chip away at as an accompaniment to our gigantic jug of margarita mix. (Another perk of sea kayaking: plenty of room for treats.) Now that I'd seen this party, I started scanning the shoreline for another spot to land—with so much room, it seemed rude to encroach on the space they'd staked out.

But as we paddled, one of their group hailed us from shore, waving us in. I squinted and recognized Rich, my friend Aleph's boyfriend, who's guided in Blackstone Bay for more than a decade. This is very Alaska, running into a friend of a friend some 20 miles into the wilderness from the nearest town.

Rich grabbed the front of my boat when we hit the beach. He and the kids he was guiding, it turned out, were camped just across the bay from us at 17 Mile, a beach I know intimately because I once dried my gear there after a days-long deluge. He chatted with us for a few minutes, offered to take a group photo of the four of us, and told us about a hike we should take up to the nearby Lawrence Glacier.

We stopped off for the hike, then paddled back to our campsite at Willard Island, having very much earned our glacial margaritas. Sometime around 10:00 p.m.—it's hard to say for sure, given that the light never truly disappears, only becoming twilight sometime after the middle of the night—we flipped the boats over and turned in for the night.

There are a number of ways to account for traveling in bear country, most of which I've touched on previously in this book. On this particular night, considering that we were on an island and likelier to see black bears than their larger grizzly counterparts, our bear-proofing plan was essentially to create a ruckus. We pulled the food and smelly items from our dry bags, condensed them, and placed them near the base of a tree set apart from our tent site, then piled noisy items—pots, pans, cups, paddles—atop our gear. If bears attempted to break into our cache, they'd make a lot of noise. This alone would likely be enough to scare them off, though we were always equipped with bear spray. (In retrospect, this strikes me as a great deal of unnecessary work, when a bear-proof canister will do the trick with far less effort.)

Sometime just before 2:00 a.m., Bix woke up, rolled over, and informed me that he had to pee. "Good for you," I told him, and reminded him to keep the tent door fully zipped, to keep the mosquitoes—the colloquial "Alaska state bird"—from invading our tent.

Moments later, his shouts brought me to life.

"You guys!" he yelled. "The tide came up!"

Hale, Angela, and I were dressed and out of our tent in seconds. Each of us was dutifully carrying a can of bear spray, all under the bleary assumption, based on Bix's shouts, that he'd been beset by a bear.

When we arrived at our cook site, though, we realized that wasn't the case at all. High tide was around 1:50 a.m.; the previous night, it had risen to within about three feet of our boats but left them untouched. Tonight, the tide had come up higher than we expected: The lower half of each boat was wet, though they wouldn't likely have been carried away by the tide.

Tides coming in higher than one expects is a fairly common problem in zones where recreators often play. Earlier that evening, I'd toddled out to a little island to take a panoramic photo when the tide started coming in quicker than I'd expected.

"Hurry," Angela called, "or you'll have to swim!"

Admittedly, I wasn't in much of a hurry, but by the time I reached the point where I'd previously crossed a calf-deep pool, I had to take my boots off to avoid overtopping them.

Some beaches in Seward, on the opposite side of Turnagain Pass, are closed depending on the tide, since hikers are liable to walk out when the water is low and then become stuck when the tide comes in. The mudflats near Anchorage are notorious for trapping people where they stand on the muddy beaches and drowning them as the water comes home to roost. The glacial silt acts like quicksand: The faster and more erratically you move, the more definitively it traps you.

Angela told me a story that cemented this idea in my head as we were driving down the Seward Highway toward Girdwood a couple of days before. (This, among many other things, is a core tenet of our friendship: We discovered early on that we both very much want to hear *all* the details, no matter how awful.) When she and Hale were in their sea kayaking class in Seattle, their instructor told them about a man who'd become trapped in the mudflats of coastal Washington, eventually necessitating a rescue via helicopter.

The chopper arrived and lowered a setup to pull him from the glacial mud. But as it pulled away, his legs remained entrapped in the mud, and his torso went with the aircraft—*he was ripped in half.* This happened in Alaska in 1961 when a man walked onto Palmer Slough, just outside Wasilla. (In that case, it happened during the recovery of his body after he drowned.)

Being torn in two by one's rescuers is a truly horrific notion, and even that feels like a profound understatement. But it's only even a remote possibility if someone can come to your aid in time. Short of that, there's a good chance waves up to 10 feet tall will engulf and drown someone stuck in the flats as the tide comes in.

We're lucky the boats didn't go far in the higher-than-expected tide. My camera was the only casualty—I'd absentmindedly left it in the center compartment of the boat.

Losing this expensive but nonessential piece of gear seemed like a small price to pay. If the kayaks had drifted away, we'd have been marooned on Willard Island (much like the 1989 party, but minus our boats) until the outfitter who rented us our kayaks noted our absence and sent a charter to look for us. The date we'd given him was still two days away, so we'd have been very embarrassed but probably not without food by the time someone came to rescue us.

The morning after our near-miss with the high tide, it was almost laughable how low the water was. Angela hiked down the beach with her bear spray to find a good bathroom spot. In Prince William Sound, as in many ocean zones, the conventional wisdom is that "dilution is the solution to pollution"; in other words, it's acceptable to poop near the tide line, as the next few days' tides will essentially flush the waste away. She came back having seen dozens of starfish. These intertidal creatures are typically seen only when there's a negative low tide; they don't like to be out of the water for more than a couple of hours.

As we loaded the boats, Bix noticed that the plastic housing on our boat's rudder had fallen apart. A tiny piece of plastic holds the rudder, the mechanism that allows you to easily steer the boat, in place—and ours was very obviously gone. He gently set the rudder in place just before we launched; it didn't take more than a few paddle strokes before it collapsed into the water.

Hale and Angela paddled up next to us; Hale, in the back, managed to pull the rudder up and set it on the stern, where we hoped it would stay for our crossing from Willard Island to the mainland.

Halfway across the mile-long crossing, I began to feel the nose of our boat pulling us to the right. I turned to Bix: "Steer us left!" I holler over the wind. He craned his neck to look at the back of the boat, then turned back around grimly.

"No dice!" he yelled back. "The rudder's in the water!"

With our mechanism for steering out of commission—and, in fact, pulling us in the opposite direction from where we wanted to go—we had to paddle doubly hard to keep our boat perpendicular to the three-foot waves. It was hard work, and by the time we arrived on the steep shoreline of Blackstone Bay, I was exhausted from paddling two right-hand strokes for every left-hand.

Eventually, we pulled the boats onto a tiny beach barely big enough to accommodate our two doubles. Famished after the effort and not sure I could continue to Decision Point, our planned campsite, without something more substantial than a granola bar, I set right to work whipping up a batch of instant mashed potatoes.

Once we'd eaten, we gathered around the end of the boat to figure out the problem. We tried a handful of solutions involving duct tape and parachute cord, none of which stood up even to the puny waves crashing on the beach. Soon, it was clear: We'd have to strap the rudder to our boat, out of the water, and steer with paddle strokes alone. This was doable but would be tough in building wind and bigger waves.

Three hours later, we passed Decision Point and arrived at Squirrel Cove, where a large group of students was in the process of vacating the luxurious tent platforms.

Rich had warned us that the weather forecast called for 30-knot winds (the on-land equivalent of nearly 35 miles per hour) on the morning we were scheduled to paddle back to Whittier. I'd been fretting about this all day—if the seas were two or three feet in the 15-knot winds of protected Blackstone Bay, what would they be like in the much more exposed channel we'd have to paddle through to make it back to Whittier?

And this was to say nothing of the boats we'd encounter: Whittier is a stop on the Alaska Marine Highway, which means enormous passenger ferries and cruise ships like the 965-foot *Coral Princess* make their way down this channel, creating waves that could easily capsize a small craft.

That night, a family of four was camped at Squirrel Cove, sharing the bear-proof metal box where we stored our food. The dad and two daughters sidled up to our little kitchen on the beach to chat. They, too, were headed to Whittier the next day; they'd been out for nine days and paddled from Icy Bay, many miles (and several serious open-water crossings) to the south of where our group had been.

The older daughter looked to be around twelve and mentioned a woman they'd encountered. This solo kayaker, probably in her seventies, the family surmised, had set out from Seward, which meant she'd paddled through Kenai Fjords National Park, where there are few beaches sufficient for landing. "For all their beauty," the National Park Service warns,

> these waters are not for beginners. The fjords are exposed to the Gulf of Alaska, with only a few protected coves. Landings often involve surf, particularly when afternoon breezes kick up from the south. Wind and rainfall can be excessive, and summer storms often push an ocean swell of three feet or more into the fjords. Inexperienced paddlers should consider traveling with a guide.

As the father and older daughter told me of their own journey from Icy Bay, the younger daughter—probably around eight years old—poked around in the tidepools, occasionally marching up to show her family a shell or rock she'd found.

If she can paddle into Whittier tomorrow, so can I, I thought. (I later told my friends of this revelation, and they laughed—of course I could do it, they said.)

The winds the next morning weren't the promised 30 knots; they probably topped out around 20, even at notoriously windy Shotgun Cove. Still, when we arrived at the harbor in Whittier— just in time to see a baby harbor seal scuttle off the rocks and into the water—I was exhausted.

Hale and Angela unpacked the boats while Bix and I set off in search of the proprietor of the outfit we'd rented from to let him know we were back and would not require a rescue. We found him in his office, which was filled with maps and photos of expeditions past. We told him about the broken rudder.

"I hope it didn't put a damper on your trip," he said, offering to refund part of our rental costs.

"No problem," I told him. "Turns out we can paddle a tandem kayak with no rudder, and we still like each other!"

He laughed, and we did, too. There are far worse ways to end a trip to Prince William Sound.

LESSONS LEARNED

- **Tell someone where you're going and when you plan to be back.** Regardless of your views on Chris McCandless and his final journey, the unassailable fact remains that if someone had known where he was, his chances of dying alone in the bush would have dramatically decreased. That's not to say a rescue is always possible, but in many backcountry destinations, there are resources in place to mount a rescue if someone is in trouble. The area where McCandless died is frequented by hunters at other times of the year, and if he'd left word of his whereabouts with a friend, someone may well have checked on him before he perished. The 1989 kayakers made a smart choice of boat charters—those folks attempted to make contact when the party didn't show up at the appointed time and place and would likely have contin-ued to do so during a subsequent weather window. On my own recent trip into Blackstone Bay, we gave the outfitter who rented us our boats a "panic time." If we'd failed to show up the morning after the day we intended to be back, he would have called our emergency contact and sent someone to look for us along our planned route. This practice offers great peace of mind not only for you, but for loved ones who might worry about your backcountry adventures.

- **Study your planned route carefully.** One of the most tragic aspects of the 1989 accident in Blackstone Bay is that it was so preventable. Twardock recommends bringing along a nautical chart to help you identify any shallow water on each day's paddle and familiarizing yourself with the tide chart to be sure you're paddling in those areas when wind and current are at a minimum. On windy days, avoid them altogether and stick to the shore. Had this party waited another day— or even paddled back up the south side of Willard Island, where there was no such shallow moraine, and attempted to cross elsewhere—the results may have been very different. When in doubt, don't get in over your head.

- **Carry sufficient extra supplies to sustain your whole party for an extra couple of days.** The amount of extra food and water you need to bring varies depending on a number of factors. How remote is your destination? How likely is the possibility of a rescue? Do some research to understand what you're up against if conditions aren't on your side, and pack accordingly. These days, thanks to finishing a few trips hungry, I never leave home for a backcountry trip without at least an extra day's ration on hand. Even if it means eating boring instant mashed potatoes, I know I'll have some calories to sustain myself if I end up stuck out longer than I expect. This extra bit of insurance helps ease worries about making it back in time; we're much less likely to make rash decisions or attempt to paddle in unfavorable conditions when we can hunker down comfortably for as long as it takes for things to improve.

- **Be prepared to self-rescue—and know when you'll become another victim.** With any backcountry endeavor, it's crucial to have a few basic skills. You should know how to treat hypothermia, for example, and apply basic first aid. (I became a Wilderness First Responder when I lived in Alaska and have kept my certification up to date in the years since; it's served me and my companions innumerable times.) One of the primary tenets of backcountry rescue is a scene size-up. In other words, ask yourself the important question: *Will I become another victim if I attempt to intervene in this situation?* If the answer is likely yes, you'll be making an already unpalatable scenario far worse; if there are two of you in the freezing water, other companions or rescuers have an ever more dire situation on their hands. Know your limits.

Epilogue

My days outside begin long before I arrive at the trail-head. The planning starts before I unload my gear from the truck, before I make the drive, even before I shuffle blearily into my kitchen and start making coffee.

Most of the time, my outings really begin a few weeks before-hand in my spare bedroom, which is also my office and sometimes, as in this case, more of a command center. They start earlier if I'm planning a multiday trip somewhere unfamiliar or logistically challenging (like another country or a long plane ride away), and later if I'm getting ready to spend a couple hours in the foothills near my house.

Say I'm planning an overnight backpacking trip in the White Cloud Mountains, a relatively remote range in the Sawtooth National Recreation Area, about three hours from my home in Boise. An outing like this—a challenging but primarily on-trail hike; an overnight requiring me to think about food and water for two days—begins a week or two beforehand.

First, the basics. I do a quick Google search to see if I can dig up any trip reports for the area I'm planning to visit. The more recent, the better. I take a hard look at the route. I download the maps to the GPS app on my phone, then sift through a stack of maps on my bookshelf to figure out if I already have a physical map of the area. If I don't, I order one online or head to the local gear shop to pick one up. There's always a chance my phone battery will die, and under no circumstances do I want to be stuck with dead reckoning as my only hope of finding my way back to the trailhead, especially now that I have written this book.

Once I have a handle on the route, a topo map gives me a pretty good idea of what I'll need to bring. Lots of vertical gain to cover? I'll want trekking poles, I'll forgo the hardback book in favor of something a little lighter, and, if I'm covering a longer distance, I'll probably want to pack more calories. Are the lakes I'll pass spring or stream-fed or glacial? Are they full of water year-round? That tells me whether I should pack a water filter, bring purification tablets, or carry all the water I'll need for drinking and cooking.

I don't have time for a long trip in the White Clouds, so I'm planning a short, logistically simple out-and-back. I'll park at the Fourth of July trailhead, hike a few miles and a few hundred vertical feet to popular Washington Lake, and follow the same route back to my truck in the morning. The trail is never very steep and the route is short, so I'm throwing in my hammock and packing a light dehydrated meal instead of something more calorically dense. Washington is a snowmelt-fed alpine lake, so I'm bringing a SteriPEN to purify my water.

With the basics squared away, I start planning for the worst. I know, it sounds morbid, but hear me out. From here, all my planning is dedicated to avoiding objective and subjective hazards, in that order.

Objective hazards are part of the natural environment we're traveling in. A cougar guarding a fresh kill, flash flooding on an equatorial island, trees falling on tents in the Boundary Waters, warming weather and resulting rockfall on Mount Rainier—all are objective hazards. We cannot control them. We can't even always avoid them; they're a risk we have to accept if we choose to push our limits outside. But if we educate ourselves about them, we can lessen our odds of falling victim to them.

Subjective hazards, on the other hand, are the ones we cause. Ironically, they're often harder to quantify or even identify—this requires a fair amount of self-awareness and honest reflection about our abilities and motivations. Subjective hazards come in a variety of shapes and sizes. Some are small and easily remedied, like getting dehydrated. Others, like skiing into a terrain trap because we've entered the backcountry unprepared to avoid avalanches, can have more immediate (and potentially dire) consequences.

This book is filled with stories of objective and subjective hazards. It's not always black-and-white. Sometimes the line between them is blurry, or one leads to another. And often, we don't get immediate feedback from our decisions.

I've probably gotten a little too close to bison in Yellowstone National Park, but I haven't been gored. Bison are an objective hazard in Yellowstone, and I know that I am supposed to stay at least 25 yards away from them. My desire to get a good photo to post on Instagram is a subjective hazard, and I will be the first to admit that it has clouded my knowledge of how to avoid them. The correct takeaway here is that I've gotten lucky. I could also take in that information and say, "Well, I've gotten too close to bison and I haven't been gored, so they must not be that dangerous." But I know that's not true. I know they really are that dangerous because every summer, I read a news bulletin or watch a grainy video shot on someone's iPhone and see that someone has very nearly been killed. I haven't experienced the feedback directly, so I've had to use other people's close calls to internalize it.

That situation is pretty straightforward: Bison are big and dangerous and don't want to be pestered, so you should give them plenty of room. Easy enough. It gets more complicated when it's personal.

Take backcountry skiing, for example. Avalanches are an objective hazard: If you choose to recreate in the winter backcountry, there's always a risk one will occur. It's your responsibility to minimize that risk by doing things like reading the forecast, understanding what constitutes avalanche terrain and when to avoid it, and so forth.

But when you throw humans into the mix, it's not quite so simple. If you're skiing with a bunch of friends, most of whom have as much as or more experience than you, and no one else points out that you're skiing directly under an avalanche path, do you notice? If you do notice—if you realize you're in the runout zone of an avalanche path, if you're not too distracted by the conversation or your own heavy breathing or wondering what the skiing will be like later—do you say anything?

If you read this and thought, *Of course I'd speak up!*, I invite you to think about this a little harder. When you're the least experienced person in a group, do you ever second-guess yourself? Do you think, *This kind of looks like those terrain trap photos in the Tremper book, but. . . . Do they* really *look like that?*

Or *This kind of looks like a terrain trap, but Emma's taken a Level 2 avalanche class, and she's usually really cautious, and she definitely would have said something if that was the case.*

Or *This kind of looks like a terrain trap, but even if it is, the avalanche danger isn't that high today, and if I bring it up I will ruin everyone's good time.*

Have you ever had any of those thoughts?

I have. I have them all the time. Reader, I second-guess myself constantly. I have spent collective years outside, had dozens of close calls, read hundreds of accident reports. I have worked in the outdoor industry for a decade. And after all that, there's still a little voice that regularly tells me I don't know what I'm talking about. I've heard of this phenomenon called impostor syndrome, but no matter whether you call it that or "that mean little voice in my head," the result is the same: subjective hazard.

If you're like me, though, doubts about the validity of your own concerns are not the only doubts. It's a chorus of doubts, of what-ifs. Sometimes they're so vivid I feel like they're unavoidable: memories of things that haven't even happened yet, of things that might not happen at all, if I'm careful enough.

For the anxious among us (the "overly sensitive," as my mother would gently put it), this presents an added challenge—how do we separate what we can control or avoid from the chorus of implausible what-ifs? How do we keep ourselves from spiraling until we never leave the house at all?

The answer, for me, is experience. I wish I had a magic spell or even a particular way of framing this that would help you get there faster, but the truth is that you just have to spend a lot of time outside and be reflective enough to learn from your mistakes.

As I get older (and gain experience), it gets easier for me to ignore the voice and speak up. It probably helps that, at this point, anyone who goes outside with me knows to expect a lecture about this or that awful thing that happened. I've also found, as I age and become more comfortable in my own sunscreened skin, that anyone who's annoyed when I insist on stopping and reevaluating the route is probably not someone whose opinion I care all that much about. Being myself is an effective way to weed those folks out.

So when I plan my White Clouds trip, I think through the objective hazards first. I check the weather and use the forecast to answer a lot of questions. Will it be hot, or cold and rainy? If the latter, is there likely to be lightning? How can I plan my route so I'm below tree line when that might happen? How many streams will I have to cross, and will there be enough rain for them to flood?

Then it's down the list: What else in these beautiful mountains could kill me? There are black bears in this area, so I'm bringing a bear canister for my food, but no grizzlies, so I'm not going to carry bear spray. I've done enough research to know that there was a huge fire in this area in 2005, which means dead trees are another concern, and I'll keep that in mind when I'm choosing my campsite and setting up my tent.

When I feel confident that I have a plan to address or avoid objective hazards, I start thinking about the subjective hazards. This particular trip is short and not particularly strenuous—it's very much in my comfort zone, which in itself can be a hazard (I don't want to get complacent), but I'm not especially worried about my fitness or my ability to perform at 9,500 feet above sea level.

Even on a short trip like this, though, it's possible to get a kind of summit fever: After a long few weeks of work, I'm *really* looking forward to sitting in my hammock and reading a book at Washington Lake. I can picture myself there: an alpine breeze rustling my sweaty hair, Bix fly-casting in the serene lake, Bodhi sniffing the breeze from the shore and keeping a watchful eye on us both. I need a break. I *need* this.

My desire to get to my goal is enough to motivate me to keep hiking when it's hot and I'm dripping with sweat. That's good; if it wasn't worth the hike, I could save myself the trouble and sit in a hammock in my backyard. It would probably motivate me to keep going if I got a little dehydrated, maybe even if I wrenched an ankle, but I don't want to sit in that hammock badly enough to stay the course to Washington Lake if I trip on a rock and break my front teeth or if a freak blizzard rolls in and I can't see the trail.

When my objective is to lie in a hammock at an alpine lake for a few hours, it's easier for me to turn around than, say, just below the summit of Mount Rainier, a climb I've been training for over the better part of a year. It's all on a scale. Whether I'm taking my dog for a quick hike in the Boise foothills or planning a weeklong river trip or climbing a volcano, I have to decide what's just an annoyance and what stands to wreck the whole enterprise. The higher the stakes, the more likely it is that an annoyance is a trip-ender: Running out of water isn't a big deal on the greenbelt, but it could lead to way bigger trouble on Mount Rainier.

Once I've sufficiently ruined everyone's fun by thinking through every possible catastrophe, I feel pretty prepared for a trip. I'll keep an eye on the weather forecast in the days leading up to my outing, but at some point, I have to accept the fact that I'm as prepared as I'm going to be. By the time I leave the trailhead, I'm relying on the sum of my experiences—the ones that made it into this book, and all the others—and what they've taught me.

I've learned a lot from my own close calls, and from the experiences of people who were less fortunate than me. The most important thing I've learned is easy to remember, and it's probably saved my life more than once. I hope you'll remember it, and I hope it does the same for you: The best way to survive an accident is to avoid having one in the first place.

ACKNOWLEDGMENTS

THIS BOOK WOULD NOT HAVE BEEN POSSIBLE WITHOUT A LOT OF mistakes.

It also would not have been possible without the input of a great many people, each of whom helped shape the stories I've just told you.

Outdoor recreators have a long history of sharing and analyzing accidents in order to learn from and avoid others' mistakes. And while I'm honored to be a part of that tradition, the unfortunate reality is that many of the folks I've described in this book did not survive to ski or hike or climb or paddle another day. This weighs on me heavily. I've tried to treat their stories with compassion, and I am deeply sorry that they're not here to tell their own stories. I hope their legacy is one of increased knowledge and understanding of the wild places we choose to recreate, so that others may stay safe and found.

Thanks also to those folks who were able to share their near-miss stories with me, and whose expert testimony I've included in these chapters. It's not an easy thing to admit when you've mis-stepped, but it can go a long way for the public good.

I am deeply grateful to the editorial team at Falcon who helped get this book into ship-shape, including Dave Legere, Ellen Urban, Rhonda Baker, and Sarah Zink. Many thanks also to my friends Hannah Brewster, Daniel Cairns, Blase Reardon, and Angela Rumsey, each of whom read chapters of this book and graciously reassured me that I was, in fact, working on a story worth telling.

I also owe a great many thanks to Lynne Wolfe for her guidance and friendship.

I will forever be grateful for the mentors I encountered during graduate school. Eeva Latosuo, Aleph Johnston-Bloom, Wendy Wagner, and Joe Stock have shaped the way I see the world and make decisions as I move through it. Alex Wilder and Hannah Brewster have been my dear friends, stalwart supporters, and, more often than I think they realize, role models, and I count myself lucky to have met them the moment I moved to Alaska.

None of the journeys described in this book was taken alone, and my companions in each chapter are mentioned by name. These stories wouldn't be what they are without those friends, and I'm grateful that each of you was gracious enough to let me tell part of our shared histories in these pages.

Being a very anxious and occasionally depressed person has given me a lot of material to write this book, but it has also sometimes made my life difficult. Allow me to take one more step toward becoming the consummate millennial: I'd like to thank my therapist. Lindsey spends much of our time together encouraging me to show myself the same compassion I feel for others, and without her patient guidance, I would spend much more of my time worrying about who was mad at me and not nearly enough time working (and not working!) on things that matter.

My parents have been endlessly supportive of all my endeavors, even when my next steps appear to be nonsensical or wildly irresponsible. They believe I am capable of accomplishing anything I set my mind to, and while that has probably made me very stubborn, I'm grateful to know I always have their vote of confidence. Anyone should be so lucky as to have parents who love them as much as mine do.

Speaking of family: I'm lucky I didn't have to look far for a role model of courage and grace, even when times are tough. My aunt

Kelly Walker is the bravest person I know. Sometimes people say I remind them of her, and this is a compliment of the highest order.

And, of course, to my wonderful husband Bix Firer, who is my champion, best friend, and fiercest cribbage opponent. I often cannot believe my good fortune in marrying someone to whom I am so perfectly suited, and who only grows more handsome and interesting with age. You believed I could write this book long before I did. There is no one else I'd rather own a boat (or, hell, share a groover) with.

BIBLIOGRAPHY

American Alpine Club. "Falling Ice, Washington, Mount Rainier." *Accidents in North American Mountaineering.* 1982. https://publications.american alpineclub.org/articles/13198205500.

———. "Falling Rock, Washington, Mount Rainier." *Accidents in North American Mountaineering.* 1986. https://publications.americanalpineclub.org/articles/13198605602.

———. "Fall into Crevasse—Snow Bridge Collapse, Washington, Mount Rainier." *Accidents in North American Mountaineering.* 1990. https://publications.americanalpineclub.org/articles/13199006302.

———. "Cerebral Edema, Washington, Mount Rainier." *Accidents in North American Mountaineering.* 1996. https://publications.americanalpineclub.org/articles/13199606503.

———. "Stranded—Lost, Inadequate Clothing and Equipment, Washington, Mount Rainier, Disappointment Cleaver." *Accidents in North American Mountaineering.* 1998. https://publications.americanalpineclub.org/articles/13199806801.

———. "Avalanche, Washington, Mount Rainier." *Accidents in North American Mountaineering.* 1999. https://publications.americanalpineclub.org/articles/13199907002.

———. "Fall on Rock, Unroped, Possibly Off Route, Washington, Guye Peak." *Accidents in North American Mountaineering.* 2002. https://publications.americanalpineclub.org/articles/13200208301.

American Mountaineering Museum. "Women in the Early Days of the Colorado Mountain Club." 29 March 2019. https://www.mountaineeringmuseum.org/blog-1/2019/3/22/women-in-the-early-days-of-the-colorado-mountain-club.

Baron, David. *The Beast in the Garden.* New York: W. W. Norton & Company, 2004.

Brown, Chip. "I Now Walk into the Wild." *New Yorker,* 8 February 1993.

Brown, Jennifer. "Death on the River: Son's Death Leads Family to Seek Reform in Commercial Rafting Regulation." *Denver Post,* 17 June 2016.

https://extras.denverpost.com/rafting-deaths/index.html. Accessed 10 January 2020.

———. "Rafting Company Was on Probation When 11-Year-Old Boy Drowned." *Denver Post*, 1 February 2017. https://www.denverpost.com/2016/09/10/adventure-company-colorado-probation-boy-drowned. Accessed 10 January 2020.

Broze, Matt, and George Gronseth. *Deep Trouble: True Stories and Their Lessons from* Sea Kayaker *Magazine.* Camden, ME: Ragged Mountain Press, 1997.

Bures, Frank. "The Sky Is Burning: Caught in the Pagami Creek Fire." *Outside Online*, 4 March 2013. https://www.outsideonline.com/1914461/sky-burning-caught-pagami-creek-fire. Accessed 10 August 2020.

Canyonlands National Park. "Water Quality." https://www.nps.gov/cany/learn/nature/waterquality.htm. Accessed 26 July 2020.

Colorado Bureau of Investigation. Case Detail: Michelle Rae Vanek. Eagle, CO: Eagle County Sheriff's Office. https://apps.colorado.gov/apps/coldcase/casedetail.html?id=1155.

Colorado Fourteeners Initiative. "14er Hiking Use Estimates." https://www.14ers.org/stay-informed/colorado-14ers-hiking-use-estimates.

Doughty, Andrew. *Hawaii: The Big Island Revealed*, 8th ed. Lihu'e, HI: Wizard Publications, 2016.

Farabee Jr., Charles R. *Death, Daring, & Disaster: Search and Rescue in the National Parks.* Revised ed. Lanham, MD: Taylor Trade Publishing, 2005.

Faulhaber, Martin, Elena Pocecco, Martin Niedermeier, Gerhard Ruedl, Dagmar Walter, Regina Sterr, Hans Ebner, Wolfgang Schobersberger, and Martin Burtscher. "Fall-Related Accidents among Hikers in the Austrian Alps: A 9-Year Retrospective Study." *BMJ Open Sport & Exercise Medicine*, 7 December 2017. https://www.ncbi.nlm.nih.gov/pmc/articles/PMC5728251. Accessed 10 April 2020.

Garden Island (Kauai, HI) Staff. "Hikers Rescued from Hanakapiai." 12 January 2020. https://www.thegardenisland.com/2020/01/12/hawaii-news/hikers-stuck-at-hanakapiai. Accessed 14 January 2020.

———. "Kalalau Trail Closed." 19 December 2019. https://www.thegardenisland.com/2019/12/21/hawaii-news/kalalau-trail-closed. Accessed 14 January 2020.

Gastaldo, Evann. "Hike Should Have Been Easy for Him. He Never Returned." *Newser*, 9 September 2019. https://www.newser.com/story/280213/experienced-hiker-sets-out-on-trail-hasnt-been-seen-since.html. Accessed 14 January 2020.

Ghiglieri, Michael P., and Thomas M. Myers. *Over the Edge: Death in Grand Canyon.* Flagstaff, AZ: Puma Press, 2012.

Griffith, Cary J. *Lost in the Wild: Danger and Survival in the North Woods.* St. Paul, MN: Borealis Books, 2006.

Harlow, Tim. "Trees Fall on Campers in BWCA; 1 Dead, 2 Injured." *Star Tribune,* 20 June 2016. https://www.startribune.com/trees-fall-on-campers-in-bwca-1-dead-and-2-injured/383629351. Accessed 10 August 2020.

Kahn, Madison. "Grizzly Attack." *Outside Online,* 5 January 2012. https://www.outsideonline.com/1787396/bear-attacks-teens-alaska. Accessed 5 July 2020.

Krakauer, Jon. *Into the Wild.* New York: Anchor Books, 1996.

Logan, Spencer, and Knox Williams. *The Snowy Torrents: Avalanche Accidents in the United States 1996–2004.* Bozeman, MT: American Avalanche Association, 2017.

Lovett, Ian, Richard Pérez-Peña, and Christine Hauser. "Flash Floods Roar through Utah, Sweeping Up Cars and Hikers." *New York Times,* 15 September 2015. https://www.nytimes.com/2015/09/16/us/utah-flash-floods.html. Accessed 15 August 2020.

McQueen, Brad. *Exposed: Tragedy & Triumph in Mountain Climbing.* Boulder, CO: Johnson Books, 2015.

Medred, Craig. "The Beatification of Chris McCandless: From Thieving Poacher into Saint." *Anchorage Daily News,* 20 September 2013. https://www.adn.com/voices/article/beatification-chris-mccandless-thieving-poacher-saint/2013/09/21. Accessed 21 August 2020.

Mount Rainier National Park Climbing Rangers, National Park Service. "Disappointment Cleaver-Ingraham Glacier: Official In-Depth Route Description." 2017. https://www.nps.gov/mora/planyourvisit/upload/Disappointment-Cleaver-Routebrief-2017_FINAL.pdf.

National Park Service. "Kayak and Boat Safety." 2 March 2018. https://www.nps.gov/kefj/planyourvisit/kayak-and-boat-safety.htm. Accessed 15 August 2020.

National Weather Service. "How Dangerous Is Lightning?" https://www.weather.gov/safety/lightning-odds. Accessed 10 August 2020.

Oaks, Robert F. *Hawaii: A History of the Big Island.* Charleston, SC: Arcadia Publishing, 2003.

Passi, Peter. "Lightning Injures Three People Camping in Boundary Waters." *Duluth News Tribune,* 20 June 2016. https://www.duluthnewstribune.com/news/4058201-lightning-injures-three-people-camping-boundary-waters. Accessed 10 August 2020.

Pauly, Daniel. *Exploring the Boundary Waters: A Trip Planner and Guide to the BWCAW.* Minneapolis: University of Minnesota Press, 2005.

Roach, Gerry. *Colorado's Fourteeners: From Hikes to Climbs,* 3rd ed. Golden, CO: Fulcrum Publishing, 2011.

Sawyer, Liz. "Girl Scouts Hurt by Lightning Evacuated from Boundary Waters in Overnight Rescue." *Star Tribune*, 27 July 2019. https://www.startri bune.com/girl-scout-group-reportedly-stranded-in-bwca-with-lightning -injuries/513277462. Accessed 10 August 2020.

Schaffer, Grayson. "Special Report: The Keyhole Seven." *Outside Online*, 24 May 2016. https://www.outsideonline.com/2072666/special-report-key hole-seven. Accessed 15 August 2020.

Scott-Nash, Mark. *Colorado 14er Disasters: Victims of the Game*, 2nd ed. Golden, CO: Colorado Mountain Club Press, 2016.

Siler, Julia Flynn. *Lost Kingdom: Hawaii's Last Queen, the Sugar Kings, and America's First Imperial Adventure.* New York: Grove Press, 2012.

Simpson, David. "Hiker Loses His Way, Dies in Yellowstone." *Jackson Hole News & Guide*, 2 June 1999: A8.

Smith, Tom S., Stephen Herrero, Terry D. Debruyn, and James M. Wilder. "Efficacy of Bear Deterrent Spray in Alaska." *Journal of Wildlife Management* 72, no. 3 (April 2008): 640–45. https://wildlife.onlinelibrary.wiley .com/doi/abs/10.2193/2006-452. Accessed 15 March 2020.

Stoner, Edward. "Hikers Surprised at Missing Women's Route." *Vail Daily*, 5 October 2005. https://www.vaildaily.com/news/hikers-surprised-at-miss ing-womans-route. Accessed 24 June 2020.

Tremper, Bruce. *Avalanche Essentials.* Seattle, WA: The Mountaineers Books, 2013.

———. *Staying Alive in Avalanche Terrain.* Seattle, WA: The Mountaineers Books, 2008.

Twardock, Paul. *Kayaking & Camping in Prince William Sound.* Valdez, AK: Prince William Sound Books, 2004.

Twin Cities Pioneer Press Staff. "Girl Scouts Not Injured by Lightning Strike." 27 July 2019. https://www.twincities.com/2019/07/26/rescuers-search ing-for-girl-scouts-struck-by-lightning-in-boundary-waters. Accessed 10 August 2020.

Whittlesey, Lee H. *Death in Yellowstone: Accidents and Foolhardiness in the First National Park*, 2nd ed. Lanham, MD: Roberts Rinehart Publishers, 2014. Print.

Yardley, William, Matt Pearce, and Nigel Duara. "Seven Hikers' Descent into Doom at Zion National Park." *Los Angeles Times*, 20 September 2015. https://graphics.latimes.com/zion-flash-flood. Accessed 15 August 2020.

Yellowstone National Park. "Bear-Inflicted Human Injuries and Fatalities in Yellowstone." 18 September 2019. https://www.nps.gov/yell/learn/nature/ injuries.htm.

———. "Hike in Bear Country." 16 July 2019. https://www.nps.gov/yell/plan yourvisit/hiking-in-bear-country.htm.

About the Author

Emma Walker was born and raised in Golden, Colorado, and has spent her adult years traveling and living around the American West and Alaska. She has worked as a camp counselor, raft guide, and avalanche educator and holds a master's degree in outdoor and environmental education. Emma works as a freelance writer from her home in Boise, Idaho.